KU-306-641

COUNTRY REMEDIES

TRADITIONAL EAST ANGLIAN
PLANT REMEDIES
IN THE TWENTIETH CENTURY

COUNTRY REMEDIES

TRADITIONAL EAST ANGLIAN PLANT REMEDIES IN THE TWENTIETH CENTURY

Gabrielle Hatfield

with an introduction by
Jean Joice

THE BOYDELL PRESS

© Gabrielle Hatfield 1994

All Rights Reserved. Except as permitted under current legislation
no part of this work may be photocopied, stored in a retrieval system,
published, performed in public, adapted, broadcast,
transmitted, recorded or reproduced in any form or by any means,
without the prior permission of the copyright owner

First published 1994
The Boydell Press, Woodbridge

ISBN 0 85115 563 4

HERTFORDSHIRE
LIBRARY SERVICE

No.
H30204 9899

Class

Supplier | Price | Date
BC | £16.95 | 11 95

EAST REGION LIBRARIES

BISHOPS STORTFORD 0279 654946
0992 623582
CHESHUNT
CUFFLEY 0707 872156
GOFFS OAK
HERTFORD 0992 583487
0992 462290
HODDESDON
SAWBRIDGEWORTH 0279 722665
WALTHAM CROSS 0992 643122
WARE 0920 462683

The right of Gabrielle Hatfield to be identified as the author
of this work has been asserted by her in accordance with
the Copyright Designs and Patents Act 1988

The Boydell Press is an imprint of Boydell & Brewer Ltd
PO Box 9, Woodbridge, Suffolk IP12 3DF, UK

British Library Cataloguing-in-Publication Data
Hatfield, Gabrielle
  Country Remedies:Traditional East Anglian
  Plant Remedies in the Twentieth Century
  I. Title
  615.321
  ISBN 0-85115-563-4

This publication is printed on acid-free paper

Printed in Great Britain by
St Edmundsbury Press Ltd, Bury St Edmunds, Suffolk

CONTENTS

Dedication

To all my friends in East Anglia
who have so generously shared with me their knowledge
of plant remedies

ACKNOWLEDGEMENTS

I am very grateful to the Folklore Society for the research grant which launched me into the field of contemporary plant medicines and to the Wellcome Trust who supported me for two years. I am indebted to Anne Williams whose work in Wales inspired me to begin this project. I would like to thank Dr David Allen of the Wellcome Trust and Dr Richard Wilson of the University of East Anglia for their help and encouragement. My thanks go too to the staff of the Norfolk Records Office. I am very grateful to my husband and family for support and understanding, and to Mrs Hazel Taylor for her care and kindness in preparing the manuscript.

Finally, I wish to thank the numerous people who have so generously shared their knowledge with me in this study. This book belongs to them.

INTRODUCTION

Jean Joice

It must be the hope of every diligent researcher that they will come across some new or hitherto concealed evidence that points the way to a different and exciting line of enquiry. Gabrielle Hatfield made just such a happy discovery while working in the Local Studies Library in Norwich when she found a reference to the work of Dr Mark Taylor which, fortunately for us, she lost no time in following up.

Dr Taylor worked as regional Medical Officer in Norwich from 1920 to 1927 and during that period collected information from local sources, mainly through general practitioners and the Women's Institutes, on many aspects of folk medicine, and it was his unpublished manuscript that gave the present author the idea for this fascinating and very soundly constructed study. Gabrielle Hatfield, a botanist, had already completed a preliminary survey of East Anglian plant remedies and realised that Dr Taylor's work, undertaken some 70 years earlier would provide a very interesting source of comparison.

In both cases the information has come from oral sources – details of plants actually used or remembered as being used by relatives or other people well known to the informants. Not surprisingly, Dr Taylor's contacts, particularly WI members, yielded more detailed 'recipes' in terms of quantities of plant ingredient and precise methods of use or application than were available from more recent sources but it is nevertheless remarkable that so much can be recalled after nearly fifty years of National Health medicine. Altogether Gabrielle Hatfield has succeeded in 'collecting' a wide variety of healing plants – some 268 compared with 86 recorded by Dr Taylor.

As one would expect, the pattern of illness has changed over the last seventy years: remedies for tuberculosis, the dreaded 'consumption', for example, are hardly mentioned in the more recent enquiry. What is odd perhaps is that the plants originally used to relieve one complaint are now being found to have more modern applications. Feverfew, which was the sovereign remedy for the 'ague', a type of malaria at one time very prevalent in the Fens, has now been found to be a excellent cure for migraine.

Similarly, the pattern of rural life has changed with villages less isolated and less dependent on their own resources. Ideas and reminiscences are less likely to be exchanged during a 'mardle' – few people have the time – but appeals for information through local radio proved extremely fruitful.

Apart from the intrinsic interest in the plants themselves and the ways in which they were used, this study offers us intriguing glimpses of rural life earlier this century and the (to us) astonishing resourcefulness and resilience of country dwellers. One story that particularly impressed me is that of the Norfolk woman who inherited a farm in the 1920s and ran it very successfully herself. When she was in her sixties she fell from the top of a stack and broke both wrists. Refusing medical help ('I haven't got time to go to hospital'), she poulticed both wrists with comfrey. Within a few weeks both wrists were healed and she had full movement in them. Not for nothing was comfrey known as 'knitbone' or 'boneset' to country people, and I too, can vouch for its amazing healing powers. A few years ago one of my favourite Jacob ewes developed a raw patch on her shoulder. It became infected and, as the weather was hot, infested with flies. The usual antibiotic sprays did nothing for her, nor did comfrey ointment, but when in desperation I macerated some fresh comfrey leaves in a liquidiser, mixed the resulting paste with pure lanolin and poulticed the wound, the suppuration ceased almost immediately and new skin was visibly forming after forty-eight hours. A neighbour who was having similar problems with her sheep tried the same 'recipe' with equal success. Incidentally, poulticing, either to apply heat or, as in this case, a plant remedy, was a popular method of treatment in earlier times and was frequently mentioned in Dr Taylor's manuscript. It was not mentioned so often in the later survey.

Happily the author has found sufficient evidence to show that the use of plant remedies, especially for domestic first aid, is still practised to a certain extent. Through her researches she discovered a Norfolk woman who has, whenever possible, treated her family's ailments with plant remedies, having collected the information about them from elderly neighbours, friends and relatives and from books. To what extent the actual plant material used is still 'local' is open to question, so many plant habitats having been destroyed by intensive farming and the use of herbicides. The pollution of roadside verges by lead makes the use of even these sources unsafe and most professional herbalists now use imported supplies.

Although Gabrielle Hatfield is mainly concerned with folk medicine used by humans, it is pertinent to wonder whether the original discovery of a plant's healing power was prompted by the instinctive selection of plants by animals according to need. The use of ivy leaves as a tonic for cattle is recorded here but I remember discovering this for myself after noticing that our Jersey cow seemed especially keen to eat ivy growing in the hedge shortly before her calf was due. When I looked this up in an old herbal it was said to be good for promoting the flow of milk. My husband clearly remembers that the horsemen on his father's farm in the twenties always tied their horses to a hawthorn bush during any break from ploughing. To the herbalist, hawthorn (*Crataegus oxyacantha*), is a safe and reliable cardiac tonic. It seems rather doubtful that the old horsemen knew this but it was certainly part of their tradition that hawthorn was good for working horses.

While it may be that the use of plant remedies in earlier times was born out of necessity in poor rural communities where doctors were few and costly, it may also have been the case that these remedies often worked better than anything the doctor could offer for good reasons that we are only now beginning to evaluate. Willow bark for example, cited as a cure for headache, contains salicin, a constituent of the modern aspirin so widely used to relieve pain and fever. Recently clinical trials have demonstrated its value in reducing the risk of stroke in patients receiving anticoagulation therapy after heart surgery.

Such 'new' evidence that the value of plant remedies is not just an old wives' tale strengthens the author's belief that folk medicine may yet be rescued from oblivion and she ends this rewarding and extensive study on the hopeful note that more clinical trials may be forthcoming. For anyone interested in plant remedies and their importance in our rural past this book is a must. I warmly recommend it – and that goes for the houseleek and cream remedy too.

CHAPTER ONE

Background to the Plant Remedies

Social conditions in rural East Anglia
seventy years ago and now

IN ORDER TO appreciate the need for home remedies in twentieth-century East Anglia, it is necessary to look back at the kind of medical help available during the nineteenth century. After the Public Health Act of 1875 and the appointment of Medical Officers of Health there were steady improvements in water supply, drainage, housing, medical inspection of school children, food hygiene and isolation of infectious diseases. All these public health measures undoubtedly led to dramatic improvements in health during the twentieth century.

However, as regards the health of the individual, and especially of the poor individual, the standard of medical care did not change as dramatically as might be supposed. For those not wealthy enough to pay for private treatment, a category which included the majority of the agricultural workers of East Anglia, there were three possible sources of aid: the Poor Law, the Friendly Societies and the Medical Clubs.

The success of the Poor Law in bringing relief was limited not only by its resources, but by the ambivalence of its administrators, who wished to make it at one and the same time an aid to the destitute and a deterrent to pauperism. The resulting public image of Poor Law aid as both a social stigma and a threat has persisted, at least in country areas, to the present day.

Discussing the administration of the Poor Law by the Board of Guardians, Hawkins, in his social study of Norwich, published in 1910, states that Poor Law medical relief . . .

> . . . is only offered, at any rate in theory, to a strictly limited class – the class who cannot or have not made independent provision against illness. It is not offered to all and sundry and it is not made too pleasant. No one who has an alternative is likely to choose the Poor Law and, except in very urgent cases, medical attendance from the Poor Law doctor is only to be obtained after application has been made to one of the relieving officers for a medical order.[1]

In her book on the Workhouse System, Crowther points out:

> The New Poor Law of 1834 . . . was based on a hard belief that the deserving and the undeserving poor could be distinguished from each other by a simple test: anyone who accepted relief in the repellent workhouse must be lacking the moral determination to survive outside it. During a century of increasing prosperity, this notion wavered and changed, though it has never disappeared. The categories of 'deserving' gradually widened, and were removed from the workhouse. Separate schools, separate hospitals, asylums for lunatics, old age pensions, health and unemployment insurance, successively peeled layer after layer of the 'deserving' away from the workhouse. By the 1920s the remaining inmates were the most 'undeserving' and the most helpless – vagrants, unmarried mothers and the aged poor.[2]

Not only was Poor Law medical aid inadequate, it was, in the minds of many, something to be dreaded, and to some extent this dread has carried over into the twentieth century, at least in rural East Anglia. For some, twentieth century hospitals are tarred with the same brush as the dreaded Workhouses and Public Assistance Hospitals: this may in part be due to the fact that many hospitals were built around former workhouses.

The following is a tale from Suffolk, which could equally well apply to Norfolk:

> The attitude of the farmworkers towards medical science has changed completely since the early thirties. Then nothing but the direst necessity would cause them to go to hospital. They had seen people going to the hospital and not returning. They therefore assumed the worst. There was a case of an old man: the doctor tried to persuade him to go into hospital for observation. He resolutely refused. 'No, Doctor, I don't hardly feel well enough to go to hospital'.[3]

It is not just attitudes which change more slowly in country regions: administrative changes are implemented far more slowly too. The image of nineteenth- and early twentieth-century medicine tends to be based on urban areas and does not accurately mirror the position in rural areas such as East Anglia.

The PEP Group Report on the British Health Services of 1937 refers to the difference in the urban and country situation. By the Local Government Act of 1929, the powers of the Poor Law Guardians were transferred to the Public Assistance Committees of the county councils and county borough councils who were given the power to 'appropriate' former Poor Law hospitals. The implementation of these changes was slower in country than in urban areas. Thus in 1937:

> In country districts few appropriated hospitals exist . . . in county areas most of the public hospitals are still administered under the Poor Law.[4]

This same report cites a more specific instance:

2

In London, for example, there is a highly developed system of public hospitals: in Norfolk, this is, except for special purposes, practically non-existent.[5]

It seems fair to say that, for the average country person living in nineteenth and early twentieth century East Anglia, the Poor Law had little to offer by way of medical assistance. Voluntary hospitals provided services for a limited number, but such hospitals were largely confined to towns and cities, and not available to the majority of the country population. In the latter part of the nineteenth-century cottage hospitals provided a limited service to the rural poor, but the numbers treated were small.[6]

From the 1830s onwards, there was a rapid growth in the membership of the Friendly Societies, particularly in Norfolk, but for many these were seen as a means of ensuring hospital treatment, should this become necessary. The Coltishall Medical Club, for example, covered ten parishes, with a population of about 4,000. Within six months of its foundation in 1836, there were nearly 800 individuals covered by it. One serious drawback of many of the nineteenth century medical clubs was that they provided cover only for the named member, and not for his dependants.

The situation changed remarkably little during the early years of the twentieth century. Hawkins, writing in 1910, estimated that in Norwich half of the adult wage-earning male population provided against sickness by subscription to a Friendly Society.[7] The usual payment in Norwich at that time was 9d (4p) a quarter for each member or 3s 6d (17½p) a year. The Norwich Friendly Societies' Medical Institute (with a membership in 1910 of about 7,000) was unusual in providing family membership: 12s (60p) a year, in 1910, would cover medical attendance for a whole family.

Outside the city of Norwich, the situation was different. Membership of local Friendly Societies was high, compared to the national average, but it provided medical cover only for the named member. Clearly to insure the whole, often large, family, would have been way beyond the means of the average East Anglian farm worker.

For someone not covered by club membership, the doctor's fee would often be prohibitively expensive. It is significant to find in the records of one rural Norfolk practice that between the years 1886 and 1894, of 1,407 patients treated, only one was a labourer, and he was charged 5s (25p) for a visit, the same as the charge for a retired army officer![8]

The medical National Health Insurance scheme, initiated in 1911, did not alter matters as dramatically as one might have expected. It did ensure that many workers were insured, and thereby entitled to free medical treatment. Wives were covered only if they worked also, and children not at all. The working family became 'panel' patients: the husband was treated free, the wife and children had to pay. The standard charge for a visit from a general practitioner to a panel patient seems to have been 2s 6d (12½p). The cost of medicine varied, usually from 6d (2½p) to 1s (5p). For a typical family of farmworkers, with a large number of children, these charges were too high to be paid except in a serious emergency. Before the 1914–18 war, farm wages were around 10s (50p) to 12s (60p) per week in East Anglia.[9]

> Working class people seldom saw a doctor because of the cost – a shilling to visit the surgery including medicine – if you were desperately ill the doctor came home; this cost half a crown old money. Mostly it was remedies mother had learned from her mother, or something a neighbour suggested.[10]

> The doctor was only called to visit homes in the case of serious accident or illness because a charge was made and this was beyond the means of many families.[11]

Financial considerations alone meant that a typical rural family in East Anglia during the first half of this century did not often call on the services of a general practitioner, even though the number of people registered with panel doctors rose from 20% of the Norfolk population by the end of 1919 to 40% in 1939.[12]

The government was made aware of the shortcoming of the National Health Insurance Act. The PEP report of 1937 pointed out that:

> The National Health Insurance System as it exists at present is, of course, nothing like a complete service. It makes no provision for medical services to very large sections of the poorer classes of the community. The largest gap affects the dependants of insured persons, mainly wives and children, but there is no provision to enable small traders and other persons working on their own, with incomes of less than £250 per annum, to get medical services.[13]

In a 1939 report of a Women's Health Enquiry Committee, there is a quote from a rural District Nurse's letter:

> It is the mother who gets left out as far as treatment goes . . . She may get the doctor for herself as well as the children if she is on the club . . . If she does not pay in she carries on as long as she possibly can without advice or treatment . . . She will not start a doctor's bill for herself if she can possibly stand on her feet.[14]

Apart from financial deterrents, there were other difficulties too in the way of a country family needing medical help. In many remote areas it was difficult to reach the nearest doctor. From the practitioner's point of view, it was difficult, time-consuming and unremunerative, to visit his more remote panel patients:

> We lived some distance from the town and it was difficult to get the doctor to visit as they had to come by horse and trap.[15]

Apart from the practical difficulties of cost and transport, there was another

4

more subtle but equally compelling reason why country people were hesitant to seek medical help except in a dire emergency. This was the attitude of the practitioners to their panel patients, as perceived by those patients. Speaking of family doctors in the area in 1925, a retired district nurse remembers:

It was difficult to move the doctors. They didn't bother too much. Time after time I would try and get a doctor to a bad case in the village but most time he never came. He would come when he thought he would. Sick people were on parish relief but the doctors ran their own medical clubs. If people didn't pay into the club, then they wouldn't get a doctor . . . there was Dr Denny who would come out any time of the day or night. He was most unusual. There were quite a few country doctors in the neighbourhood but none of them did this. They were important folk then and the villagers were a bit nervous of them. As for the old family doctor – he was for the old families, if you know what I mean.[16]

There were undoubtedly some panel doctors who did their best to scale down charges to their poorer patients. Here is a story of a Suffolk practitioner in the early years of this century:

The father of a man who worked for me contracted tuberculosis and was a long time dying. For years Dr Wilkin attended him and never sent in a bill. When he was unable to walk, Dr Wilkin somehow found a wheelchair for him. When this patient ultimately died, the bill was sent in. The widow told me it was five pounds – for all that work – for all those many years. She said to Dr Wilkin: 'Doctor, I'll never be able to pay this.' 'Oh yes you will, don't be worried. Pay it just when you feel you can – no hurry – I know you'll pay me.' And so she did in the end.[17]

It is of course difficult to assess how common such kindness was; but a system which depended on the philanthropy of the individual practitioner was bound to result in inadequate medical care of the poorer members of society.

In a *Report on the British Health Services*, published in 1937, it is mentioned without comment:

Sometimes middle-class patients go to the doctor's front door and working class patients to the surgery door.[18]

The obvious 'them and us' division which existed between the panel doctor and his poorer patients would undoubtedly have further deterred many poor patients from seeking his help. Add to this the very strong streak of independence which still characterises many country-born East Anglians, and one begins to understand why even the scant medical services that were available to the less well-off were often not utilised.

The story is told of a lady in Forncett End, Norfolk, who, in the 1920s inherited a farm, and proceeded to confound the predictions of fellow-farmers by running it very successfully herself. One day, when she was in her sixties, she

Comfrey
Symphytum officinale L.

fell from the top of a stack and broke both wrists. The helpers on the farm tried to persuade her to go to hospital:

> 'Hospital? I haven't got time to go to hospital!' was the reply. She proceeded to poultice both wrists with comfrey from her garden. In a few weeks both wrists were healed and she had full movement in them.[19]

This characteristic of self-reliance was probably not confined to the East Anglian rural worker. A survey undertaken by the Ministry of Labour in 1937 showed that the rural worker spent less than his urban counterpart on the doctor, dentist, nursing attention and medicine.[20] This in part of course reflects his smaller income.

Another extreme example of East Anglian independence comes from Essex. The author's informant recalls how, in 1948, he was discussing the newly formed National Health Service, with a local lady called Jan:

> Old Jan was quite a character! A small, wizened woman, her features bronzed with many years exposure to all types of weather. Her movements, despite her years, were quick with an agility more common to someone half her age, which was widely rumoured to be in the region of seventy-five years. Seeing Jan potato-picking, fruit-picking, or tackling any of the jobs which had to be done on the farms where she worked, one would think she was, at the most, forty years old.
>
> Once, when asked the reason for her health and agility, she said 'Hard work, good food and clean living'. Locally, however, she was considered somewhat akin to a doctor, and many residents in the locality would consult Jan when they felt unwell, rather than call or go to visit a doctor
> . . .

Yarrow
Achillea millefolium L.

Several years have gone since Jan passed over, but, five years before her death I had the good fortune to be in her company, and to be entrusted with some of her 'old-fashioned remedies'. It happened that she was potato-picking for us, and about the middle of the morning it started raining, stopping potato-lifting. We all adjourned into the barn, and the conversation turned to the newly instituted National Health Service. Jan insisted, 'we don't need all these 'ere doctors, we can look after ourself'. She then straightway launched into a list of complaints and their treatment.[21]

The existence of local 'experts' on home remedies was probably widespread in country areas throughout the first half of this century, but unfortunately it is very difficult to find out about them, since no records were kept, no money changed hands, and their fame was spread entirely by word of mouth. Time and again, speaking to elderly country people, they have recalled people who, like Jan, were automatically turned to in times of illness.

In some instances, one individual was famous for treating one particular ailment:

The rector knew a thing or two about medicine, even more than Liz Button who could cure burns.[22]

One lady in a Norfolk village became locally famous for her ointment for 'festered fingers', a complaint that was common and painful in agricultural Norfolk where a cut from an agricultural implement could so easily go septic. Every week, this lady visited the local butcher where she bought lard. This was taken home and clarified (boiled and the scum, etc. discarded). It was then spread on copper pennies in a thin layer, and the pennies were spread in her

7

Feverfew
*Chrysanthemum
parthenium (L.)Bernh.*

cellar until a good thick growth of fungus was obtained. This was scraped off with a knife into small pots, and sold at a penny a pot. Apparently it worked really well, and would presumably have contained anti-biotics, as well as copper salts which are known to have an anti-fungal action. This was of course long before the days of official anti-biotics.

This particular anecdote is unusual in that it is the only instance which the author has come across which involves payment. The lady concerned presumably had at least to re-imburse herself for the lard.[23]

Another lady, of Essex origins, became well-known for her first-aid ointment. She had a large family herself, and when her children were small found that the ointment she made from yarrow was extremely useful, so each spring she made up a batch for use during the year. Again, word soon spread and before long she found it necessary to make up larger and larger batches so that she had enough to give to her friends as well. This lady moved to Norfolk and brought her recipe with her.[24]

In more recent times, a lady living at Flordon Common in Norfolk regularly makes up an infusion for 'flu' from the water mint growing in the stream near her cottage. She says that she has given it to 'ever so many people', and added the interesting observation that 'when you have a remedy, you don't use it yourself'. In this particular case, the remedy is one remembered from her grandmother, who herself knew the uses for 'every plant on the common'.[25]

In addition to people famous for one particular remedy, there were also locally famous experts on a variety of home remedies, like Jan described above (see p. 7). Mothers of ill children would automatically consult the local expert, who in some cases was also the local midwife, trained or untrained. Such people were held in great respect by adults, and sometimes viewed with awe if not fear by children.

One lady who has lived all of her eighty-plus years in the village of Rockland St Mary, Norfolk, remembers vividly two unmarried ladies who shared a cottage in the village when she was a child. They spent much of their time gathering plants from the hedges and fields, and on their kitchen range there was always a concoction brewing. The village children were slightly afraid of these old ladies, whom they clearly regarded a bit like witches. Their parents, however, regularly called at the cottage for help and for medicines.[26]

A lady now in her sixties describes a colourful character from her childhood in Moulton, Norfolk. This old lady, who always wore a black trilby hat, visited all the households with children each spring, bringing with her a tonic of thick syrup with little green apples bobbing about in it. Every child, protesting or otherwise, was given a dose. Nobody now seems to know what was in it.[27]

In the North Norfolk village of Wiveton there lived in the early years of this century another forceful personality still vividly remembered by people who were children then. One man, now in his seventies, recalls how she rescued the whole family when they were laid low by a particularly vicious variety of 'flu'. The brew they were given tasted foul, but it did the trick.[28]

Many of these glimpses of the 'wise women' of East Anglian country life are tantalisingly incomplete. However, in the case of Granny Davis, midwife in the village of Wicklewood, we have a much more complete picture, thanks to the writing and the accurate memory of F.C. Wigby, author of *Just a Country Boy:*

> Granny Davis was a wonderful old lady. The lady on the advert for *Robinsons Starch* was exactly like her: when it used to be on the bill hoardings it always reminded me of her.
>
> She brought most of the children in my village into the world and laid out those who had passed on. As there were no chapels of rest, the corpse was placed in a coffin, placed on trestles and left there until the funeral. In summertime, Feverfew was placed around it and also on the lid as it was taken to the place of burial. Many seeds of the Feverfew fell off en route and that is why the plant is, or was, frequently found in many village churchyards, mainly on the north side where the paupers were buried, or those who had committed suicide . . .
>
> Granny made wonderful homemade beer from hops, Horehound and malt which was in great demand in hot weather. For nursing mothers she made up a decoction of sifted bran, oats and skim milk which, when boiled helped them to recover.[29]

Some of Granny Davis' plant remedies are described in Chapter 2.

Rather less commonly, the local expert on home remedies was a man. Elizabeth Harland in her *Diary of a Country Housewife* describes a market gardener who, in his Suffolk village, was more famous for his plant remedies than his garden produce:

I recall the cheerful grin, the bright succory-blue eyes, and the Father Christmas beard of Henry Knights, pottering about in the wooden shed which housed a car nearly as old as himself, and bundles of the herbs he collected at appropriate seasons.

Many were the stories told of invalids who visited him for the first time driven in a dog-cart or pony-trap, so 'set fast' with rheumatism or lumbago that they had to be helped down from their conveyances. Sent away with a bunch of dried 'harbes', plus instructions on how to use them, their next call would be paid on foot, sometimes from a distance of several miles.

(Of the plants that he used), a few he grew in his garden. But most he collected from hedge and common during the summer months, waiting until each was dead ripe and at its best, always choosing a day just before the moon reached its zenith for the gathering.[30]

Some of Henry's remedies are described in Chapter 2.

No consideration of remedies would be complete without a reference to wart cures. These fall into a rather different category to other East Anglian remedies, and, since they rarely employ plants, will not be considered in great detail here. As one retired schoolteacher from a Norfolk village pointed out, warts 'really deserve a book to themselves'. He himself had frequently come across the practice of 'buying' warts, usually for a halfpenny each. The person gifted with the ability to buy warts counted the warts and then paid accordingly. The warts frequently disappeared. One day the schoolteacher decided to have a go himself at buying the warts on one of his pupils. It worked, he said, like magic, but to his chagrin, a little while later he found himself the owner of warts on his own hands which refused to go away, and he resorted to liquid nitrogen treatment at the local clinic! There are numerous examples of local wart-charmers in East Anglian villages. Sometimes the 'gift' is confined to one individual, sometimes a whole family is renowned for the ability. There are still people around today who practise the art of wart-charming with apparent success.[31]

It seems, judging by the frequency of tales of wart-charmers, that warts were a more common complaint earlier in the century than they are today. One elderly man recalls how in his youth he was employed to drive the baker's van. To his dismay, his hands became covered in unsightly warts, which appeared also on his face. His job was in jeopardy and he had to do something to get rid of the warts. He had heard tell of a man living nearby who could 'charm warts', but he felt very doubtful himself about the whole thing. In desperation he visited the man, who carefully counted all the warts, and told him to go home and by morning they would have disappeared. They had![32]

In addition to wart-charmers, there were numerous ways of ridding oneself of warts, most of which involved rubbing the warts with an object which was then buried. As it decayed, so the warts would vanish. Objects used included a piece of raw meat, preferably stolen. How far such methods were actually used, and to what extent they were simply traditional tales, is not clear. Most people who mentioned them had not actually tried them, only heard tell of them.

In contrast, there were and are a number of simple plant remedies for warts which country people did use, and still do today. These were a cheap and effective way of getting rid of the complaint, and it is noticeable that no ritual or ceremony was involved: simply the application of the plant. The plants used in this way are described in Chapter II.

We have seen how, in many areas, there was one or more local 'expert' on various ailments. In addition to this, most country people had their own basic system of first-aid. Many farms were too remote to acquire help quickly at the time of an accident so, again, it was necessary to rely on friends and neighbours:

> Once a harvester came at twilight for first aid. He had not heard the boy holler 'Holdjer', and a pitchfork had pierced his hand as he caught at sheaves being tossed into the wagon. My father washed the wound and filled it with salt. How that man danced round our kitchen![33]

The story is told of a north Norfolk fisherman who came into his local pub looking drawn and miserable, with his hand bandaged. The publican asked him what had happened, and he explained that while gutting a fish he had got a bone buried in his hand, and had been unable to remove it. The publican sent one of his customers out to the field behind the pub to fetch a large dock leaf and a cow pat. The fresh cow manure was plastered on the man's hand, which was then wrapped in the dock leaf. The patient complained of awful pain in his hand. 'Never mind, drink up', he was ordered, and a pint put in front of him. Some half an hour later, the poultice was removed, and there was the white end of the cod-bone sticking up. It was quite easily removed![34]

Fresh cow pats were quite commonly used in this way, for treating animals and humans. A Norfolk postmaster recalls his father curing a foal with a badly cut leg, using fresh cow dung and a potion which he made. The leg healed without a scar.

Another frequently used first-aid application for cuts was cobwebs. This same postmaster remembers a friend working in a barn cutting his fore-arm badly on a bill hook, and calling for cobwebs with which he wrapped his arm. The arm healed well.[35]

A lady brought up on the Halvergate marshes remembers her granny's treatment for cuts. Bad cuts were wrapped in cobwebs, minor ones were swished around in a pail of cold water. The cut was then bound up and left bound for a week.[36]

From Essex comes this vivid account of first-aid in the country in the early years of this century:

> My mother-in-law was a wonderful person, she was married in the last century at the age of 20. Her husband was nineteen and he worked on a farm earning 10s (50p) a week and they lived in a small cottage. Through the years they had twelve children which the midwife delivered, sometimes in candlelight. Mother never had a doctor, as you had to pay two shillings

and sixpence (12½p) every time he came. When my husband was a boy he had to chop the wood for the fires. One day he chopped the top off his thumb. Mother washed it well, then put the piece back on the thumb and bound a lily leaf on. She got a bandage and wrapped it on so securely it had to stay on for a week. When it was taken off the thumb was all healed up and he never had a scar.[37]

Such examples could be multiplied indefinitely, but these few will serve to illustrate the necessity for self-reliance in times of illness in the country parts of East Anglia during the first half of this century. It is against this background that the remedies to be described in the following pages must be viewed.

CHAPTER TWO

Remedies

I N THE COURSE of researches at the Local Studies Library in Norwich, the author had the good fortune to come across a reference to the manuscript work of Dr Mark Taylor.

Dr Mark Taylor was born in 1871, the son of Thomas Taylor, surgeon in Bocking, Essex. He qualified at St Bartholomew's Hospital in 1894 and practised at Helston in Cornwall. In 1915 he moved to Acton, where he was a surgeon at Acton Hospital, and a member of various medical committees.

In 1920 he became the first full-time regional Medical Officer and worked in this capacity in Norwich from 1920–1927, when he moved to Southampton. After retirement he went to live near Liverpool and continued part-time work for the Ministry of Health. He died at Formby, Lancashire, in 1942.[1]

During his years in Norwich, Dr Taylor collected information for a book that was never actually published entitled 'Magic, Witchcraft, Charm-cures and Customs in East Anglia'. At the end of a paper he presented to the Folklore Society he stated:

> Now I think what I have told you will show what a mine of good stuff exists in East Anglia. My great regret is that I should have been transferred to another part of the country before I had sunk more than a few trial shafts . . . If I am unable to publish the book, I shall hand over all my manuscripts and notes to the Central Library at Norwich where they will be available to anyone who is prepared to carry on the good work.[2]

As the title of Taylor's work suggests, he was interested in all aspects of fok medicine. However, since the present author, as a botanist, is particularly interested in plant remedies, it is this aspect of Dr Taylor's work which is mainly discussed in the following pages.

In presenting some of the remedies collected by both Dr Taylor in the 1920s and by the present author in the 1990s, it seems logical to arrange these according to the ailment for which they were used.

This classification immediately presents some anomalies: there are certain conditions, such as 'ague', and consumption for which the incidence, treatment and prognosis has changed very dramatically during the last seventy years.

13

These illnesses were widespread and life-threatening in East Anglia during Dr Taylor's life: now they are virtually absent (ague) or rare (tuberculosis) and in both cases, curable by modern treatment. It is hardly surprising then to find a relative dearth of 'home remedies' in the 1990s for these conditions – in fact, the only remedies recorded recently are clearly memories rather than remedies in current use.

Because these conditions form a group apart, they will be described first.

Ague

In the past, this term was used to describe almost any type of fever, but it seems that, particularly in the fens, malaria was still prevalent until the early years of this century.

The remedies which Dr Taylor recorded for ague include marshmallow sweets (reported by Dr Randall, Boston, Lincolnshire), and cobwebs:

> Cobwebs, mixed with pure butter and made into ordinary-sized pills, have been known to cure a very bad case of ague, one or two taken nightly.
>
> (Blythburgh WI, Suffolk)

Dr Clapham, of Thorney near Peterborough, wrote to tell Dr Taylor that opium was used extensively in the fens for ague. His letter is of such intrinsic interest that it is quoted here:

> As regards drugs the fen people used opium very extensively for ague – in my opinion with greater success than quinine for the variety of 'ague' met with years ago in the district. (It is curious that this disease is practically non-existent at the present time. I have not seen a case of malaria in twenty years which has arisen in the Fen, whereas in my father's earlier years in practice, and my grandfather's and great-grandfather's, and also his father's (all in the same village – Thorney), it was a very prevalent complaint. The same applies to Stone.

In Mark Taylor's handwriting, the following is added:

> Dr Clapham told me that he had heard his grandfather say that in his day a fenman would not thank you for a pint of beer unless you put a dose of laudanum in it or a pipe of tobacco unless doped with opium.

The late Dr Wales of Downham could remember the time when on market days the chemist would have five or six Winchester quarts (five pints) of laudanum on his counter, and any woman coming in to market would take home sixpenny-worth for the week's supply for the family. Opium seems to have been used as a universal panacea.[3]

That this state of affairs continued on into the early decades of this century is confirmed by Frederick C. Wigby, author of *Just a Country Boy*. He was born at

Wicklewood, near Wymondham, Norfolk, in 1912 and was brought into this world by Granny Davis 'who acted as an unpaid midwife at all confinements' Mr Wigby has told the present author:

> Granny Davis was a wonderful old lady . . . she brought most of the children in my village into the world and laid out those who had passed on . . . Laudanum was freely available in those days. Granny used it quite a lot and regularly put a drop in babies' bottles, as did many a mother.[4]

It comes as no surprise that the present quest for home remedies in East Anglia turned up no specific remedies for 'ague'. Even the name seems to have died out early in the century.

Rolf, the 'King of the Poachers' in his fascinating book, *I Walked by Night*, says:

> They used to be a lot of ague in them days in the marshlands, Marsh Fever as they used to call it, but I have not heard of a case for many a year, except in men comen home from India or some such part. The cure was hot beer with mustard seed boiled in it, which was counted a fine powerful remedy.[5]

Enid Porter records the use of willow-bark tea for malaria in the fens.[6] The present author has come across this remedy for headaches (see p. 40).

John Glyde, in his book *The Norfolk Garland*, claims that:

> In the Fen district of Lincolnshire a spider covered with dough and taken as a pill is a charm for ague in which people place great faith, and I find that to swallow a spider or its web when placed in a small piece of apple is an acknowledged cure in Suffolk.[7]

This is repeated, almost word for word, in Walton Dew's book, *A Dyshe of Norfolk Dumplings*.[8]

Is this another instance where 'They books, they get it all wrong!' (see p. 61)? These may well be inaccurate versions of the remedy described by Blythburgh WI. There is always a danger in folklore studies of recording the more bizarre and strange, sometimes at the expense of accuracy. This is pointed out by Newman and Wilson in their fascinating study of folk medicine in Essex and Lakeland:

> When isolated examples of folk cures are quoted by writers on local folk-lore, there is a tendency to select and emphasise the more spectacular types of treatment and to ignore the simpler but more generally used cures as being less interesting, even if they are really typical of folk medicine.[9]

This is a caveat that any workers in the field of folk medicine must bear in mind.

Consumption

This was a widespread and dreaded killer in East Anglia until the advent of sulphonamide drugs in the 1940s.

One Norfolk man in his nineties has described the difficulties of life in his childhood. He was one of five children. His mother died of consumption when he was three. 'Food was difficult', he says – quite an understatement. Their staple diet was stewed turnips, carrots, onions, with the addition, when they were lucky, of a free bullock's head, which would feed the family for a week.[10]

At the beginning of the century, orthodox medical treatment for tuberculosis had not progressed far since the days of William Buchan. Koch's discovery in 1882 of the tubercle bacillus had not yet borne clinical fruit, and the only beneficial treatment available was fresh air. It is small wonder, then, that the home remedies too for tuberculosis had stagnated since the eighteenth century, and still consisted largely of broths made from slugs and snails.

Among the plant remedies recorded by Taylor is beer made from nettles. This, according to Dr Randall of Boston, Lincolnshire, was regarded as a 'specific' for tuberculosis.

Mrs S.B. of Norwich told Dr Taylor that a decoction of lungwort (*Pulmonaria*) was used for treating consumption.

Red roses, crushed with sugar, were recommended in the 1920s by Huntingfield WI (Suffolk) for coughs and spitting of blood.

Evidently, there were some strange beliefs concerning the spread of tuberculosis. Mrs B., in a letter to Dr Taylor, wrote:

> A man or woman who is consumptive may not sleep with the husband or wife, as they two being one, both will get it. But with this one exception a man never gives it to a woman nor a woman to a man, therefore if one of the partners is consumptive, the girls sleep in the father's room, and the boys in the mother's room. As a Spitl (?Hospital) Poor Visitor I have done my best to persuade people to give up the practice, but have never succeeded. In one case the father was the patient and the little girl who slept with him caught it, the guardians sent her to a country home for three years – the parents never could understand how she got it. The father is now dead. The mother is a tailoress, and all the time her husband was ill, for many years, did work in the room where her husband was.

Presumably the latter was out of necessity, rather than choice; accommodation was probably so limited that rooms had to be shared.

Another insight into beliefs surrounding consumption is provided by information given to Dr Taylor by Miss Shaw from Heckington, Lincolnshire:

> My father says it is or was a well known fact that anyone living in a slaughter house or cow house will never have consumption (it is rarely a butcher is known to suffer from that illness).[11]

With hindsight it seems strange that such ideas remained prevalent long after

Juniper
Juniperus communis L.

the discovery of the causative agent of the disease. Presumably the reason for this is that there was still no good cure available: where an illness is incurable, any straw will be grasped! In the course of this work it has been noticed that the only ailments for which some theory of disease has been suggested are those, such as rheumatism, which are commonly regarded as incurable.

Abortion

For obvious reasons, it is difficult to find out information concerning methods used unofficially to procure abortions in the early years of this century. No effective means of birth control was available, and without doubt abortion was used in lieu: since this is a highly sensitive subject, people are on the whole unwilling to talk about it.

However, Dr Taylor came across four plants used in Norfolk in the 1920s to procure abortions. The first of these is savin, 'generally put into the teapot with ordinary tea'. This is *Juniperus sabina*, a known abortifacient, used since the time of Pliny. Another species of juniper is a constituent of gin: a well-known way of trying to terminate an unwanted pregnancy was to drink plenty of gin.

'Fairly large doses of pennyroyal' were also used to bring about abortions (Mrs S.B., Norwich): this plant, *Mentha pulegium*, is again a known abortifacient.

Dr Calder of Lowestoft informed Dr Taylor that saffron tea was used to bring about abortions. Saffron consists of the pistils of the flowers of *Crocus sativus*, and used of course to be cultivated in East Anglia. Joseph Miller writes:

> The best saffron in the world is grown in England being cultivated in Essex, Suffolk and Cambridgeshire.[12]

The plant gave its name to Saffron Walden in Essex.

The plant is a known 'emmenagogue', a term applied to drugs which provoke

17

menstruation, and often it seems used as a more acceptable term than abortifacient.

The fourth of Dr Taylor's abortive agents is of considerable interest, and was at first difficult to interpret. There is a note, with no source given, that 'Heira Peika or Hikey Pikey' was used to bring about abortions. This, it seems highly likely, is a corruption of the eighteenth century 'hiera picra':

If the menses cease all of a sudden, in women of a full habit, they ought . . . to keep the body open. This may be done by taking once or twice a week, a little rhubarb, or an infusion of hiera picra in wine or brandy.[13]

The 'Sacred Tincture' or Tincture of 'Hiera Picra' was composed of aloes, virginian snakeroot and ginger.[14]

Snakeroot is *Aristolochia serpentaria L*, which, along with various other species of *Aristolochia*, has long been used as an emmenagogue. Mrs Grieve mentions in her *Modern Herbal* that the species *A., clematitis*, is found in England 'usually near old ruins, as if it had been cultivated for its medical use, as an aid to parturition'.[15]

Interestingly, this plant was reported to be growing 'as freely as a weed' in the garden of Carrow Abbey, Norwich: this building was originally a Benedictine nunnery.[16] The plant was first recorded as growing there in 1793 by Rev. Mr Salton, and was still growing there in 1968.[17]

A slight diversion is necessary here, because there is evidently some doubt concerning the identity of the saffron used to procure abortions. The true saffron, as grown in Saffron Walden, is *Crocus sativus*, a member of the *Iridaceae*. However, in East Anglia, the quite different plant, savin, *Juniperus sabina L.*, a low-growing, evergreen shrub and member of the *Coniferae,* is known by the name 'saffen', presumably a corruption of 'savin', and a name which could easily be confused by the listener with 'saffron'. The confusion is rendered worse because both plants were used to procure abortion, both in humans and in animals.

George Ewart Evans in *The Farm and the Village* quotes Harold Smart, a West Suffolk horseman, as saying:

We had all Suffolks at that time, and we looked after them well . . . I doctored a lot of them myself. I used bearsfoot, saffen, garden tansy, ferns from out of the bank. Bearsfoot was for condition, and to keep their coats looking well. Saffen was a wonderful herb for the coats too . . . I gave saffen to my horses in two ways. I boiled it in an old pot, then I strained the liquid and then sprinkled it on their food, each horse getting the right amount. I also baked it, dried it, and made a powder of it.

George Ewart Evans identifies 'saffen' with Tusser's savin, i.e. *Juniperus sabina L.,* and goes on to say:

This herb saffen was called the threepenny bit herb by some horsemen because the dosage for a horse was the amount that would cover a silver threepenny piece. It was highly dangerous to use and was in fact poisonous if given carelessly. Some horsemen maintained that it has contraceptive qualities and if a mare was given saffen she would never get in foal.[18]

Compare this with an article which appeared in the *East Anglian Magazine* in December 1975:

I was talking one summer evening to the late Bill Mead as he pottered around in his front garden. I remarked on a small shrub that stood in the middle plot and asked him what it was. Bill, an ex-horseman replied: 'That's saffron. You must have seen it growing round churchyards many a time and there's no harm now in telling you what we used to use it for. If you had a good working mare in your stable and the gaffer wanted her in foal and you didn't, you'd mix some dried saffron leaves in her grub and the stallion could keep coming round all he liked but she'd never click for a foal. Not only that, it made her coat shine.'[19]

The present author has unfortunately not been able to trace the writer of this letter, but it seems likely that the plant described here is, once again, 'saffen' or savin, *Juniperus sabina*, rather than saffron. One would be unlikely to describe saffron, with its grass-like leaves springing from a single corm, as a small shrub. Furthermore, it is the stigmas of the saffron flowers that were and are used medicinally and for culinary use, and not the dried leaves.

The 'sweet saffron leaves', mentioned in *The Horse in the Furrow*, by George Ewart Evans, and used for shining the horse's coat, may well be another example of the use of *saffen* rather than saffron.

In a hand-written notebook, belonging to a local ratcatcher called Jimmy, and written about 1850, there is a recipe for a powder 'To make a horse feed'. It includes bitter ginger and 'suffen' – presumably another version of the East Anglian 'saffen'.[20]

This example, although trivial in itself, has been described in some detail because of its more general importance in studies of this kind. The identity of the plant being described is not always easy to establish with certainty. The present author has found that the use of actual specimens of the plant or, failing this, of accurate botanical illustrations, sometimes helps to clarify the situation. Obviously this is only possible where data is being collected first-hand and, moreover, it entails repeated visits to the informant which, however enjoyable, can be very time-consuming. However, the moral of the 'saffen' story seems to be that, if there is any doubt surrounding a plant's identity, it is better left uncertain than guessed. As other ailments are described, further examples of the difficulties involved in identifying the plants involved will be given. (See, for instance, under skin conditions, boils, rashes – houseleek, 'marsh dock', 'secension'.)

Having given this caveat, it does however need to be pointed out that, even though the names given in domestic plant remedies are almost invariably their common names, rather than their scientific ones, in the vast majority of cases there is virtually no doubt concerning their identity. This is partly due to the fact that most home remedies use very common and well-known plants.

Returning now to the plants used in this century to procure abortion, Pennyroyal, *Mentha pulegium*, has continued in use, although how widespread is its use is difficult to establish. The staff of an old people's centre in Essex discussed their early memories of contraception and abortion with a group of four women, average age eighty, in 1990.

> Married or single, should unwanted conception take place, physical exer-
> cise was often the first option. The women would be urged to walk, big
> strides were best, jump down stairs, stretch and lift heavy objects. For sale
> were compounds such as Widow Welsh's Female Pilles and Pennyroyals,
> said to work only in the early stages of pregnancy. We got the impression
> that taking this course of action was seen as a necessary evil, becoming a
> form of birth control in itself. Premature labour was also hoped for by
> drinking gin (for its juniper oil) and slippery elm. It would seem that these
> remedies often failed and more mechanical means were sought. When
> recalling the risk of illness and death surrounding back-street abortions, the
> staff were drawn back into social circumstances which were outside their
> experience.[21]

Analyses of *nostrums* for amenorrhoea, carried out for the British Medical Association and published in 1912, showed that many contained pennyroyal.[22]

The only other present-day means of procuring abortion which has come to light in the present study is the use of ergot from mouldy rye. This was recalled by a woman, now in her seventies, living at Wicklewood in Norfolk.[23] Ergot is, of course, the original source of the drug *ergotamine*, still used officially for inducing labour. How widespread was its unofficial use in East Anglia, and elsewhere, in the early years of the century? This is probably an impossible question to answer.

It seems likely that the relative scarcity of records of plants used to procure abortion is largely due to the sensitivity of the subject, and the unwillingness of most people to talk about it.

Boils and Abscesses
Several elderly people have commented that boils seem to have been commoner in their youth. Be that as it may, there were certainly a lot of domestic remedies used in East Anglia to bring boils to a head and to heal them. Many relied on heat or suction (bread poultices, a heated neck of a bottle), and these will be described in a separate volume of household remedies. Of the plant remedies used, the following were collected by Taylor in the 1920s:

Groundsel poultice and boil it, and then soak bread in the boiled water, and put it on the boil. (Eyke WI, Suffolk)

Parsley poultice and also a cabbage leaf is excellent for boils or pushes. (Blythburgh WI, Suffolk)

For bad breasts, poultices made of houseleeks.   (Ancaster, Lincs.)[24]

Groundsel poultice appears again in the 1990s. A lady now living in Foulsham, Norfolk, recalls how, in the 1930s, her uncle was off work, sick, with lots of boils on his arms. There was no sickness benefit, so money was very scarce. A gipsy called at the door, selling lace and pegs. Her aunt answered the door and the gipsy said she looked worried, and what was the matter? The aunt replied that she had scarcely any money and explained about her husband's illness, and that she certainly couldn't afford to buy anything. The gipsy made a bargain: 'Buy something, and I'll tell you a remedy that will cure your husband.' This was agreed, and the remedy was as follows:

Wash groundsel, remove just the leaves, make them into a flat parcel in a piece of linen, old sheet, etc. Pour on boiling water, squeeze out the parcel and put it on the boil.

Uncle's boils were cured, and never returned. This happened at Hayes in Middlesex. The informant now lives in Norfolk, and has passed on the remedy to others. She has found it useful in treating cuts and grazes, as well as an acutely swollen and inflamed big toe.[25]

Rolf, the King of the Norfolk Poachers, in his book *I Walked by Night*, recalls that his grandmother used 'secention' for boils: this is a Norfolk name for groundsel, *Senecio vulgaris*.[26]

Cabbage leaf has likewise been used for the treatment of abscesses within living memory in Norfolk. One lady described how she developed a breast abscess while nursing one of her children. She picked a large cabbage leaf from the garden, removed the midrib and wrapped the portions of leaf around her breast, inside her bra'. The abscess cleared quickly and completely.[27]

Houseleek poultices were recalled as useful for treating boils and abscesses.[28] Other plant poultices used include onion[29] chickweed,[30] and 'Pick-a-cheese', the common mallow (several records from Norfolk).[31] In this latter remedy, the flowering shoots were boiled to a sludge, which was then used as a poultice. Pick-a-cheese is an attractive country name for the common mallow, *Malva sylvestris*, based on the resemblance of the fruit to old-fashioned cheeses. The author had not come across this name before, and on this occasion it was necessary to gather the plant and take it to the informant before its identity was established with certainty. The name 'pick-cheese' is quoted by Britten and Holland in 1878 as in use in Norfolk and Hertfordshire for the fruit of *Malva sylvestris*.[32] The present author has heard this name used, throughout Norfolk, for the whole plant. An ointment made from marshmallow and chickweed was

Mallow
Malva sylvestris L.

also used.[33] Two single records are of interest: from Hoxne, Suffolk, comes the memory of using chopped 'bulfers' (puff-balls)[34] to cure boils, again in the form of a poultice, while from Braintree in Essex comes this vividly recalled memory:

> When I look back to that distant past I think what an important part home remedies meant to country folk . . . My mother and father kept a corner of their large garden to grow a great many herbs – coltsfoot, horehound, hedge woundwort, as well as all the culinary herbs . . . My mother's favourite was the hedge woundwort and many boils, carbuncles and the like were brought to a head with poultices made from the leaves.[35]

The hedge woundwort is presumably *Stachys sylvatica*, the use of which as a poultice is referred to by Grieve.[36] Both this species and *Stachys sylvatica* (Gerard's clown's woundwort) are still used today as wound-healers in herbalism.[37]

Dock was used in two ways for the treatment of boils and abscesses. The first method, recorded from Bedford, was to wash and boil the roots of common dock, and drink the water in which the roots had been boiled, a wineglassful a day.[38] The second involved the use of dock seed:

> While a bread poultice was used to draw a suppurative wound or a boil, a more interesting and lasting cure was given me by old Mr David Windley of 'Sellet's Green'. This was to gather a handful of the ripe seed of dock (*Rumex obtusifolius*) and to infuse same in some boiling water and then leave to cool. The liquid was then strained and a wineglassful drunk over several days. This cure I was able to put to the test, and in three cases it worked. Carbuncles were treated by Mr Frank Lodge from 'Sokens' by the taking of some nutmeg – this he assured me had cured him.[39]

Burns and scalds

Dr Taylor in the 1920s came across two household remedies for burns. The first came from Blythburgh WI (Suffolk):

Take some fresh primrose leaves, wash well and dry thoroughly. Soak in linseed oil, and place on the wound. Will heal in two or three days.

The practical details supplied here suggest that this was a remedy actually used. It is interesting to compare this with an entry in an eighteenth century kitchen book belonging to the Harbord family, and now in the church of St Peter Mancroft, Norwich:

Oil and honey spread on primrose leaves to take the heat out of burning.[40]

This is clearly the same remedy as that still being used in Suffolk nearly two hundred years later.

The other burn remedy which Taylor records is the use of raw scraped potato applied thickly (Eyke WI, Suffolk). The potato is still used in this way today. There are records of its use in this way from Walcott (Norfolk),[41] Docking (Norfolk), Diss (Norfolk), and from Bircham WI (Norfolk). (See Appendix.)

Other recently collected remedies for burns include an ointment made from marshmallow.[42]

An interesting remedy for burns comes from Salhouse, Norfolk: alder leaves were lightly crushed and laid on burns. In this instance there was no doubt about the identity of the plant used; the locality has numerous alder trees, and it was definitely alder and not elder leaves that were used. This appears to be a 'one-off' remedy; the author has been unable to find any other records for it, although alder leaves are still used by some country people, placed inside the shoes to relieve tired feet. Possibly the use of alder in treating burns is an example of a purely empirical remedy, and may be evidence of the continuing development of plant remedies in country areas.[43]

Two other plants have been used in East Anglia within living memory for treating burns and scalds. Raw onion was rubbed on to 'take the fire out'.[44] Presumably it replaced one fire with another!

The other remedy is of considerable interest in that it employs a plant which is of only local occurrence and is highly toxic, namely the thorn apple (*Datura stramonium*). This plant still occurs as a week of cultivated land, turning up in gardens from time to time. The green, prickly fruit was boiled in pork fat to make an ointment used for inflammations, burns and scalds.[45]

This remedy is unusual in employing a relatively uncommon plant, and one generally known to be toxic. As far as can be ascertained, it was not used internally. It is interesting to find that Gerard recorded this use of thorn apple, which he used himself with great success. He tells us:

The first experience came from Colchester, where Mistress Lobel, a merchant's wife there, being most grievously burned by lightning, and not

23

finding ease or cure in any other thing, by this found help and was perfectly cured when all hope was past, by the report of Mr William Ram, *publique notarie* of the said towne.[46]

Here then is an example of a seventeenth-century domestic remedy from Essex, still in use in domestic medicine in rural Norfolk in the twentieth century. To what extent its survival depended on its appearance in Gerarde's *Herbal*, we shall probably never know!

As far as can be ascertained, the thorn-apple was not used in domestic medicine internally. The only other contemporary use of it found in East Anglia was in the treatment of asthma (see Appendix).

The last twentieth-century domestic remedy recorded for burns comes from Norfolk, although it originated in Ayrshire, Scotland. The informant was brought up by his grandmother, who had a reputation for being able to cure almost anything. Mr M. recalls how she treated a friend of his with a badly scalded face. Mr M., then a small lad, was sent to gather ivy leaves from the stable wall. These were crushed in a mixture of vinegar and olive oil and applied as a mask to the injured boy's face. The burns healed without any blister.[47] It is interesting to compare this with the recipe in the old *English Leechbook of Bald*.[48] This recommended the tender twigs of ivy boiled in butter for treating sunburn.

All the informants who provided the present author with burn remedies were careful to stress that these home remedies were only used for relatively minor burns. It was fully recognised that more serious burns needed professional help.

The remedies found for sunburn will be considered under the heading of skin complaints, see p. 50.

Cancer

This term is here used in a lay rather than a strictly medical sense, since clearly people who used home remedies early in this century would themselves have insufficient knowledge to differentiate strictly between 'benign' and 'malignant' tumours.

Dr Taylor's remedies, collected in the 1920s, include the use of a hemlock poultice (Huntingfield WI, Suffolk). Unfortunately details of how the plant was used are not provided. It was used in Greek and Arab medicine for the treatment of tumours. In more recent times, Grieve tells us that,

among the moderns, Baron Storch was the first to call the attention of medical men to its use, both externally and internally, for the cure of cancerous and other ulcers, and in the form of a poultice or ointment it has been found a very valuable application to relieve pain in these cases.

This was in the late eighteenth century.[49]

Carrots were also used for treating cancers, again in the form of a poultice

(Huntingfield WI, Suffolk). Instructions for the use of 'narrow-leaved dock' in treating cancer are slightly more precise. This remedy was supplied by Baconsthorpe WI (Norfolk) in the 1920s. The dock was to be boiled, and the growth steeped in the resulting liquid. The growth was then poulticed with the boiled dock.

It is impossible to establish with certainty the identity of this 'narrow-leaved dock', but it may be *Rumex conglomeratus*, which is common and does have narrower leaves than many of the other common species of dock.

The only internal remedy for cancer recorded by Taylor is a decoction of celandine, used especially for liver cancer (Dr Ball, Lowestoft). Again, the identity of the plant is uncertain, but it is probably the greater celandine, *Chelidonium majus L.*, a member of the poppy family, that was used in this way rather than the unrelated small celandine (*Ranunculus ficaria*). The greater celandine is a toxic plant, although 'no harmful effects from therapeutic doses have been established'.[50] The juice has been used topically in treating malignant tumours of the skin.[51] It is interesting that Grieve in her *Modern Herbal* records that:

> Celandine is a very popular medicine in Russia, where it is said to have proved effective in cases of cancer.[52]

The relatively poisonous nature of several of the plants used in the home treatment of cancer forms an exception to the general rule that most domestic remedies contain non-toxic plants. This is not surprising: cancer being such a serious condition, people would have been prepared to risk the use of even toxic plants in an effort to achieve a cure, or alleviation from pain. This was presumably more true in the early part of the century when cancer treatment in orthodox medicine did not have a great deal to offer.

The remedies collected in East Anglia in recent years will now be described.

A poultice of houseleeks (*Sempervivum tectorum*) was used in Essex for 'cancerous growths'.[53] This plant was very widely used throughout East Anglia for a wide variety of ailments (see earache, skin conditions, etc.), and is still used today in country areas. As has been pointed out above, the term 'cancerous growth' does not necessarily mean malignant growths in the strict sense of the word, and some of the growths so-treated may have been, in medical parlance, benign.

However, there is no doubt concerning the medical diagnosis in the following cases. One lady recalls her uncle having a cancer on the lip, which he removed using dandelion juice (*Taraxacum officinale*).[54] From Hemsby in Norfolk comes the story of a man diagnosed at the Norfolk and Norwich Hospital as having facial skin cancer. While waiting for treatment, on the advice of a local gipsy friend, he tried rubbing it with the pith of a banana. By the time his hospital appointment came up, there was no trace of the cancer and, even though an excision was performed, no malignancy was found. Later, a similar growth appeared; again he used banana, and again it disappeared without trace.[55]

From South Walsham in Norfolk comes the story of a man who apparently cured himself of a facial cancer using a poultice of violet leaves.[56] This use of violet leaves is recorded by Grieve:

Of late years, preparations of fresh violet leaves have been used both internally and externally in the treatment of cancer.[57]

The British Herbal Pharmacopoiea (1983) records that the sweet violet (*Viola odorata*) has been used both internally and externally for treating cancers,[58] and that a related species, *Viola striata*, has been shown to have anti-tumour effects in mice.[59]

The last domestic remedy collected recently in Norfolk comes from Swannington, and is of interest in that it was regarded purely as palliative rather than as a cure. Mrs H. recalls how her grandfather suffered from throat cancer for several years before his death. As a small child, she was sent by her grandmother into the fields to gather wild mushrooms. These were stewed in milk, and the resulting liquid was given to grandfather. Apparently it was very soothing. The actual mushrooms themselves were given to the little girl.[60]

Both awareness and incidence of cancer have increased in Britain since the beginning of the twentieth century. One might be led to expect an equivalent rise in the number of home remedies used. However, orthodox treatment has improved dramatically, and it is probably true to say that few people in recent years would have recourse to home remedies for the treatment of such a frightening illness.

That modern science should take note of such domestic remedies such as are recorded is well illustrated by the fact that the Vinca-alkaloids currently used with great success in the treatment of childhood leukaemia were developed from a South American species of Periwinkle during the second half of this century. Two hundred years earlier, in Suffolk, the use of poultices of *Vinca* was recommended for breast lumps.[61]

Chilblains

Most chilblain remedies, both in the 1920s and 1990s, did not involve the use of plants and will not therefore be discussed in detail here. (The commonest remedy was to dip them in urine in the chamber pot: it is ironical to find that wealthy eighteenth century members of the Harbord family, of Lowestoft, used wine instead.)[62] Thrashing chilblains with holly until they bled was a drastic but widespread remedy, recorded by Taylor from Huntingfield in Suffolk.

An 'excellent cure for chilblains' was contributed by the Orford WI in the 1920s:

Melt half a pound of lard in a saucepan, add 2 oz rosemary, 1 oz ?balm,

4 oz wild southernwood, half a pound of roses, garden variety, 7 different kinds, more tea roses than others, boil all together for twenty minutes, then strain and use when cold.

In the 1990s, people still recall beating chilblains with holly till they bled. This was recorded both in Norfolk,[63] and Essex.[64] Another remedy from Essex also involved the use of holly, but this time as a chilblain ointment. The berries were powdered and mixed with lard.[65] The same informant recorded an ointment for chilblains made from lard and the juice of deadly nightshade (*Atropa belladonna*). A lady from Essex[66] recalls rubbing onion on chilblains. Also from Essex comes the use of the red berries of bryony. These were crushed, and rubbed on chilblains.[67]

Doubtless chilblains were a more common affliction in the past when few houses had central heating. Many elderly people recall the misery that they caused.

Chilblains were the curse of wintry weather, and we hobbled to school with rags wrapped round our toes. Girls sometimes shuffled along in older brothers' boots. One remedy my father remembered involved beating raw cracked toes with holly, and the next stage was to rub the toes with snow! Was this treatment to help the circulation? After school, feet, stockings and socks too, were soaked in warm water until the toe-rags became unstuck from the broken chilblains.[68]

Constipation

'Keep your bowels open, your pecker up and your faith in the Lord.' This is a North Norfolk recipe for a healthy life![69]

Many elderly country people reminiscing on life in their childhood have commented that, on the whole, 'they were a healthy lot'. This they attribute mainly to a simple but wholesome diet. Homemade bread in particular is often singled out as a healthy item of their diet. George Baldry writing in *The Rabbit Skin Cap*[70] points out:

Most villages had their own windmill and ground their own corn, very often making the meal into bread with no bran taken from it, so the people were more healthy as it is more laxative than the fine flour of today.

A lady born at Reedham in Norfolk in 1903 recalled very vividly her mother's baking days. She was one of fourteen children, seven girls and seven boys. On Tuesdays and Fridays mother made bread, so father got up extra early to light the fire to warm the bread oven. On baking days, as a treat, bread rolls were split open, a lump of cheese popped inside, and the rolls returned to the oven for a minute or two. Then they were eaten, and the lady can obviously almost taste them still after all these years. She pointed out that, though they were hard up, their food was wholesome and free from chemicals.[71]

It is tempting to speculate that constipation was not as common a problem among country people in East Anglia in the early years of this century, and that this could account for the fact that only one remedy for constipation (cloves boiled in water and steeped overnight, Huntingfield, Suffolk) appears among Taylor's notes from the 1920s.

Against this argument, many elderly people today, who were themselves children in the 1920s, recall all too vividly the weekly dose (always administered on a Friday for obvious reasons!) of brimstone and molasses, or liquorice powder, or senna infusion, or syrup of figs.

> Great store was put in 'purifying the blood' and 'purging the system'. Cabbage water and nettle tea fulfilled the former and liquorice powder, the latter. The routine nature of this weekly dose led to queues forming outside the lone toilet every Saturday morning. No wonder the children attempted to dodge this ritual, even if it meant some poor unfortunate taking a double dose on the promise of extra pocket money.[72]

Among the plant remedies collected for constipation in the 1990s are several pieces of dietary advice, e.g. eat boiled onions,[73] or a drink of rice and raisin 'tea'.[74] Chamomile tea was also recommended.[75] Perhaps the most interesting advice comes from Whissonset, Norfolk, where children used to chew the fruits of 'pick-a-cheese' or common mallow as a laxative.[76] This certainly sounds a more pleasant remedy than the sulphur and molasses which many elderly people still recollect with disgust.

Coughs and Colds

Not surprisingly, a large number of domestic remedies were found for coughs and colds, both by Taylor in the 1920s and by the present author in the 1990s. Self-treatment is still the first reaction of most people to these common ailments. Probably the cold was regarded more seriously in pre-antibiotic days, because of the danger of pneumonia which could easily prove fatal. There were numerous patent cough and cold remedies and there still are today. Of the plant remedies, the commonest seems to have been onion, used in a variety of ways.

Taylor recorded the use of a hot onion poultice for a cold on the chest (Eyke WI, Suffolk). For a head cold, the same group used tea made from chamomile or sage (Eyke WI). Drinking a pint of hot elderberry wine on going to bed was probably a very pleasant way of banishing a cold (Eyke WI). Hot infusions of peppermint leaves, or of Rosemary were used by Orford WI (Suffolk) sage, lemon and honey was recommended by Blythburgh WI.

From Wilby in Norfolk comes the following recipe for colds:

> Get some ground ivy when it's in blossom, dry it, keep it till the winter, then boil it in some water. Use the tea (ground ivy is *Glechoma hederacea*).

Horehound (White)
Marrubium vulgare L.

Dr Stacy from Great Yarmouth wrote to Dr Taylor to tell him that an infusion of yarrow flowers (*Achillea millefolium*) was used to treat bronchitis.

An infusion of horehound (*Marrubium vulgare*) was also used to treat coughs and colds (Wilby WI).

Two interesting cough mixtures were supplied by Huntingfield WI in the 1920s:

Elicampaign roots dried and grated in a spoonful of sugar,

Root of marshmallow dried and mixed with raisins, boiled and strained of half the water then let it stand.

'Elicampaign' is presumably elecampane, or horseheal (*Inula Helenium*) the root of which was formerly candied and eaten as a cough sweet. The plant is still used in modern-day herbalism for the treatment of coughs.[77]

Recipes for two gargles for a sore throat were supplied by Huntingfield WI in the 1920s. The first consists of an infusion of currant leaves, the second is the juice of boiled sloes.

Of the cough and cold remedies collected in the 1990s, by far the commonest was the onion, used in a variety of ways. Here is an 'Old Fashioned Remedy' from Essex:

1 lb nice onions chopped; 1 lb demerara sugar; 1 lemon. Chop onions, mix sugar and juice of one lemon. Leave in cool place for a day or two and strain off syrup into a container.

Excellent for bronchitis or chest cough. I have used this since I was young and I am now 92 years old.[78]

Various versions of this remedy turn up all over East Anglia. Some still recall vividly the unpleasant taste of the onion brew. In the case of a persistent cold:

> The hot lemon gave way to rings of onion or turnip sprinkled with brown sugar; spoonfuls of the resulting liquid were given three times a day. I still shudder at the memory of turnip and sugar, but my parents believed the worse it tasted, the better it was for you. Diet at this time would be gruel, hot bread and milk and occasionally a boiled Spanish onion.[79]

Onions as gruel, as a poultice, or as juice for a cough medicine were used very widely (see Appendix). A variation on this theme was the use of roasted shallots for a cold.[80] Infusions used as cough mixtures included feverfew,[81] mullein,[82] cowslip,[83] and horehound (several records). The horehound was sometimes infused in wine, sometimes made into beer. The root, candied, is still available as a cough sweet. The smoking of coltsfoot (dried flowers and leaves) was used as a cure for bronchitis, as well as being a cheap substitute for tobacco.[84] This use of the plant goes back to the times of Pliny, and gave the plant its botanical name of *Tussilago*.

The water in which horseradish root had been boiled was used as a cough medicine,[85] and also used for treating catarrh.[86]

Gargles for sore throat included sage with vinegar and honey,[87] and marshmallow root with honey,[88] whilst a 'tea' or syrup made from blackcurrants was used as it still is today as a soothing drink. The root of comfrey was chewed for a sore throat.[89]

Elderberry wine was used as a treatment for coughs, colds and 'flu', and was a much more palatable cure than many (see Appendix).

Coughs were also treated with a decoction of the bark of wild cherry,[90] or of cherry, plum and sloe bark.[91] Coughs in animals were treated with boiled linseed and bran.[92]

An interesting remedy for influenza and heavy colds comes from Flordon in Norfolk, and consists of an infusion of water peppermint, drunk hot. This plant is abundant in the marshes near where the informant lives, and she has recommended it as a remedy to innumerable friends, but adds the interesting observation that she doesn't use it herself: 'If you have a remedy, you don't use it yourself.'[93]

Whooping Cough

Whooping cough seems to have had its own domestic remedies. Taylor records the use of garlic, rubbed into the feet and hands (Wrentham, Suffolk) or placed in the socks (Boston, Lincs.) or made into an ointment (Huntingfield, Suffolk). The following recipe comes from Cringleford, Norfolk in the 1920s:

> A handful of blackcurrant shoots, half an ounce black liquorice, 3 lumps of sugar, 1 pint of water. Well simmer for 1 hour for whooping cough.

Other remedies included figs soaked in gin (Huntingfield, Suffolk), a decoction of robin's pincushion (a gall that grows on the wild rose) (Brundall, Norfolk), houseleek (Wivenhoe, Essex), a syrup of mulberry and castor oil (Wilby, Suffolk), and an infusion of marigold flowers (Wilby, Suffolk). The following remedy for whooping cough also appears among Taylor's notes, but no source is given:

> Mouse's ear is a weed or herb that grows in grassy places, dried and later been thoroughly dry is made into a tea is used for children in cases of whooping cough.

This probably refers to *Pilosella officinarum*, a plant still used in herbalism today for whooping cough and bronchitis.[94]

The last plant remedy recorded by Taylor for whooping cough is to 'carry the babe through a field of beans in blossom, walking up and down the rows to let the child inhale the powerful scent' (Sproughton, Suffolk).

This sounds much pleasanter than the alternative and widespread treatment for whooping cough which was to inhale the fumes from fresh tar at roadworks or the fumes from gasworks.

Inhaling the perfume from bean flowers was also reported in 1990 as a cure for whooping cough.[95]

Other plant remedies for whooping cough collected by the present author include the juice in which parsnips have been boiled[96] and the use of mistletoe for 'hoping cought' reported by the King of the Norfolk poachers in *I Walked by Night*.[97] How the mistletoe was used unfortunately is not known. The use of garlic for whooping cough is described by a lady from Essex, now in her nineties:

> I was born 1910, and when I was a child at the age of four years I was put to bed unwell by my mother who told me I had whooping cough and I was to stay in bed. My mother looked up the remedy book called *Common Ailments* to see what to use; it said Garlic Pods to be crushed to a pulp and put on lint then apply to the soles of the feet; it was *not* to touch the skin. Lots of folk refused to believe this cure and laughed about it but she had the last laugh when a peaceful night was had and the next morning there was no sign of the whoop.[98]

This lady would have been about ten years old when Taylor collected his remedies. This is one clear instance of the overlap in time between Taylor's collection of plant remedies and that of the present author.

It is of interest that, both in Taylor's collection of remedies and in the present collection, the remedies for whooping cough are distinct from those for an ordinary cough. Most coughs associated with colds are viral in origin (and therefore do not respond to modern antibiotics) whereas whooping cough is bacterial in origin. Garlic has known antibacterial action, and may well have helped.[99]

Time and again, the author has been impressed with the vindication by modern science of many of these simple plant remedies. It is a pity that so few of them have as yet been investigated in depth, a situation which is discussed further in the concluding chapter.

Cuts and Wounds

In a primarily agricultural region, farming accidents were common. As everyday emergencies, one would expect to come across numerous remedies for cuts and wounds, and such proves to be the case. There are no fewer than five versions of the following recipe among Dr Taylor's notes:

> Take the flowers as they fall of madonna lilies (white), dry in the sun, put in wide mouth bottle, cover with brandy. Will stop bleeding and heal cuts very quickly, will keep years.   (Yoxford WI)

A Fressingfield (also Suffolk) version of this remedy is an ointment made by stewing lily leaves in pork lard, and has the note added 'variety of lily apparently not important' (Dr F.C. James). However, most versions specify either petals or leaves of madonna lilies.

The other plant remedy for wounds collected by Taylor is as follows:

> Take ascension, called in towns groundsel, boil for ten minutes and apply as a poultice.   (Baconsthorpe WI, Norfolk)

The Norfolk name for this plant is of interest: in Norfolk it is sometimes called 'sesension', sometimes 'ascension'. Both are evidently corruptions of the plant's botanical name, *Senecio*. Britten and Holland in their 1878 *Dictionary of English Plant Names* give 'sencion', 'sension', or 'senshon' as names recorded for *Senecio vulgaris* from Essex, Norfolk and Suffolk.[100] As we have seen on p. 21, this selfsame remedy is still in use in Norfolk for the treatment of boils.

The remedies for cuts and wounds collected in the 1990s are numerous. The use of madonna lily, usually petals, but sometimes leaves, and always steeped in brandy, has been recorded from Norfolk, Suffolk and Essex (see Appendix). An interesting variant of this is the use in Essex of a dock leaf treated with brandy for application to cuts.[101]

Other leaves used to treat cuts were houseleek (*Sempervivum tectorum*),[102] used in Norfolk, and leaves of wild rose or briar (Essex).[103] Puff-ball spores were a well-known styptic for cuts, used for both humans and animals. Apparently most farmers kept a puff-ball hanging up in a shed for use as needed; barbers in Norwich did likewise![104] This use has been recorded in both Norfolk and Suffolk; a lady from Great Yarmouth particularly recommends them to stop the bleeding from broken varicose veins.[105] There is a particularly vivid story from Hemsby about a dog that severed an artery: a tourniquet and the dust from a 'Smokey Jo', as it is called in parts of Norfolk, saved the dog's life.[106] Other names for the puff-ball include 'bolfer' or 'bulfer' and 'devil's soot-bag' (Suffolk). George Ewart Evans recorded the version 'bullfice' which he interprets as a rendering of the seventeenth-century 'bull-fist'.[107] Britten and Holland in their 1878 dictionary give 'bullfeist' as a Norfolk and Suffolk name for this fungus and 'bulfers' as a common Norfolk spelling, while devil's snuffbox is quoted as another country name from various counties.[108]

Bruised geranium leaves were sometimes used to treat cuts.[109] This use of geranium leaves is also recorded in the Fens by Mary Chamberlain in her book, *Old Wives Tales*.[110]

Of great interest is the use of dried and powdered hemlock leaves to treat cuts. The informant lives at Hoxne in Suffolk. While he was working for the River Board at Great Waltham in Essex, he noticed that when the riverside vegetation was cut back, there was a scramble to collect the shoots of hemlock. He was puzzled by this, knowing the plant to be poisonous, so he asked what it was for, and was told that the leaves, dried and powdered, were used for treating cuts.[111]

Deep cuts were sometimes treated with horse-radish root, which apparently helped them to heal.[112] This use is also recorded by Enid Porter in Cambridgeshire.[113]

Ointments for cuts were made from elderflowers (Norfolk, Suffolk) and from comfrey root (Kenninghall, Norfolk; Colchester, Essex) (see Appendix). Of particular interest is a remedy imported into Norfolk, but originating in Essex. The lady concerned lived originally in Dovercourt, Essex. She had a large family and inevitably a lot of cuts and grazes to attend to:

> My late father, who was born in 1900 and was the third of nine children, told me of an ointment made by his mother to treat all cuts, grazes and injuries that had drawn blood. She would take yarrow plants – the whole plant including the flowers and the roots, and wash them well. They were then chopped up finely and boiled to a pulp in a little water, pushed through a sieve and the resulting paste then mixed into purified lard. This ointment was used on the many cuts and grazes suffered by her large family and my father said that they all healed up cleanly and quickly. People used to come to the house and ask for some of the ointment regularly.[114]

Yarrow has been used throughout the world for a variety of ailments, and has been shown in recent years to possess local anaesthetic as well as haemostatic properties.[115] Its common name of 'nosebleed' implies another of its uses.

Another treatment for cuts comes from a lady in Essex, born in 1917:

> We were lucky enough to live in the country and to have a grandmother who understood the healing properties of plants . . . Our grandmother, wearing what must have been the last of the proper sunbonnets (I have never seen another), gathered goosegrass which she cooked and fed to the goslings, hence the name, but a pad soaked in the liquid and bandaged over a wound was supposed to help the tissue to knit quickly. Goosegrass is the

Goosegrass
Galium aparine L.

weed that children call Sweethearts, probably because of its propensity to cling. We were not asked to gather it as the seeds were too tiresome to remove from our clothing.[116]

A young woman living in Suffolk has developed her own first-aid ointment, known in her family as 'greenstuff'. Equal parts of ground elder and comfrey are boiled up in vegetable fat and bottled as an ointment for cuts and grazes.[117] Ground elder, often known as goutweed, was used in the treatment of gout and sciatica, and was recommended by Gerarde for this. Most of us today know it mainly in its role of enemy to the gardener, so vividly described by Gerarde. It

. . . groweth of itselfe in gardens without setting or sowing, and is so fruitfull in his increase that, where it hath once taken root, it will hardly be gotten out againe, spoiling and getting every yeere more ground, to the annoying of better herbes.[118]

It is nice, then, to know that it still has its uses!

The last plant remedy collected in recent times for the treatment of cuts presents a botanical puzzle, and illustrates the difficulty which sometimes, though not often, surrounds identification of a plant cited in a remedy.

A lady living in Quy in Cambridgeshire described a 'heall-all tree' that grew in her garden when she was a child. It was a little tree or bush, with leaves that were shiny on one side. One side of the leaf was used to heal cuts, the other to 'draw puss'.[119] This was described in the 1980s and is strikingly similar to the following entry found among Taylor's notes of the 1920s:

For Blood-poisoning
A plant called heal-all leaf. The wrong side of the leaf for drawing the

Rose-root
Sedum rosea (L.)Scop.
Rhodiola rosea L.

matter out, and when clean apply the right or up part of leaf to heal. Change frequently.   (Blythburgh WI, Suffolk)

The same remedy was described in 1990 by a lady, born in 1917, and brought up with her grandmother's cures:

'Ee-law' leaves were used on one side for healing and on the other side for drawing such as boils or whitlows although whitlows had their own cures in whitlow grass or whitlow whort. Ee-law, I discovered eventually, should have been heal-all.[120]

These three remedies must surely refer to the same plant, but the botanical identity of it has not yet been established with certainty. The garden near Quy is now a housing estate, so that particular 'heall-all tree' will never be seen again. The likeliest identity for the plant seems to be the rose-root (*Sedum rosea*) which, we are told in Britten and Holland, is

. . . often to be met with in gardens, where it is sometimes called heal-all, for the leaves are applied to recent cuts of a slight nature.[121]

Diarrhoea

Two interesting plant remedies are recorded by Taylor from the 1920s:

Boil the green leaves from a mulberry tree and drink the infusion. A sure cure.   (Dr F.B., East Harling, Norfolk)

This seems to be a 'one-off' remedy. The mulberry is better known for its fruit, which are mildly laxative.

The second remedy is as follows:

> Grate a ripe acorn into warm milk and give to the patient, brandy 2 oz, arrowroot 1 oz. (Woolverstone WI, Suffolk)

The use of powdered acorn for diarrhoea was recorded in Suffolk by the photographer Emerson,[122] whilst earlier still (late seventeenth century) grated oak bark was used by the Harbord family for the treatment of diarrhoea. Oak bark, with its high tannin content, is still recommended for acute diarrhoea.[123]

The use of acorns, rather than oak bark, would obviously be simpler as a home remedy, and may have come about by the observation that acorns fed to pigs are 'binding'. Grieve comments:

> In many country districts acorns are still collected in sacks and fed to pigs; but these must be mixed with other vegetable food to counteract their binding properties.[124]

One of the plant remedies for diarrhoea collected in the 1990s is an infusion of ribwort plantain leaves (*Plantago lanceolata*), recorded from Kenninghall in Norfolk.[125] The origin of this remedy is not known. Some species of plantain (though not this one) are used medicinally for their mucilaginous seeds, whilst an infusion of common plantain leaves is recorded by Grieve as being used for diarrhoea and piles.[126]

The other recent plant remedy comes from Terrington St Clement School (Norfolk) and consists of the leaves, roots or fruit of the strawberry, infused.[127] The leaves are recorded as being 'mildly astringent'.[128] Grieve also refers to the use of both roots and leaves in diarrhoea.[129]

Earache

This is nowadays one of the commonest childhood complaints which General Practitioners are called upon to treat.

In the past, onion in various forms was by far the commonest first-aid plant treatment for earache. It was recorded by Taylor from four Suffolk branches of the Women's Institute, one Norfolk doctor, and one Lincolnshire school. The only other remedy recorded was 'a quid of tobacco' (Lowestoft).

In the 1990s, onion still seems to reign supreme as the most common plant remedy for earache. Sometimes a hot poultice of onions was applied:[130] sometimes a small roast onion was placed in the aching ear (numerous records). A variation on this theme comes from Trunch, in Norfolk, where roasted shallots were used to treat earache.[131] Onions, like garlic, contain allicin, which has known antibiotic properties.[132]

The juice of houseleek (*Sempervivum tectorum*) was sometimes squeezed into a sore ear.[133]

Finally, an infusion of wild poppies was used to relieve the pain of earache.[134]

This remedy comes from a family living in the country, and it is interesting to compare with the recollection of a lady now living in Essex, but brought up near Smithfield Market in London:

> Whenever we had earache we used to get a poppy seed head from the chemist (2d) and mother used to bind that round our ear.[135]

Both the wild poppy (*Papaver rhoeas*) and the cultivated opium poppy (*Papaver somniferum*) possess pain-killing properties, although opium itself is not present in the wild poppy.[136]

Sore Eyes

Taylor recorded the use of eyebright (*Euphrasia officinalis*) for inflamed eyes (Huntingfield WI, Suffolk).

For a 'film across the eye', a correspondent from Beccles in Suffolk told Taylor that an infusion of celandine was used. Whether this was the greater or the unrelated lesser celandine is not stated, but it is highly likely to have been the greater celandine (*Chelidonium majus*), of which Grieve says 'in milk it is employed as an eye lotion, to remove the white, opaque spots on the cornea'.[137]

A variety of plant remedies were recorded in the 1990s for eye disorders. Cucumber juice was regarded as 'very good for the skin and the eyes', applied as a lotion.[138] It is a common ingredient of cosmetic facial masks.

For swollen, inflamed eyelids, crushed watercress gathered from the marshes was used.[139] The juice of houseleeks (*Sempervivum tectorum*) was dripped into children's eyes to soothe conjunctivitis.[140] An infusion of chamomile flowers (*Chamaemelum nobile*) was used to soothe sore eyes,[141] as was an infusion of eyebright.[142]

Of great interest is an infusion of the petals of 'sore-eyes' used in Whissonsett, Norfolk. The informant seemed surprised that I did not know this name for bird's eye, or speedwell, and she described how her grandmother infused the little blue flowers to make a soothing eye-bath.[143] It seems to have been the very common germander speedwell (*Veronica chamaedrys*) that was used in this way.

From Essex, the use of an infusion of ground ivy (the whole shoots were boiled up) was described by a lady now in her nineties,[144] a use that dates back at least to Gerarde's time. The latter recommended it mixed with celandine and daisies.[145]

Finally, from Essex, comes this pleasant-sounding remedy:

> In the herb garden we grew chamomiles, so that we could have chamomile tea. But my mother would also collect some of the flower heads and with rose petals and my favourite cornflowers, would boil them for just about a minute, then place them between the folds of a clean handkerchief and put the compress over her eyes to relieve them from tiredness.[146]

Germander speedwell
Veronica chamaedrys L.

Compare this with the following entry in *The Gunton Household Book* (late seventeenth century, Suffolk):

> Break Spectacles water
> Take blew bottles yt Grow in ye Corn gathered with their Cups and bruise as many as you please, steep them in a good quantity of snow water for 24 hours then distill them in an ordinary still very moderately, and keep ye water. This is most wonderfully effectuall not only to Cure most of ye infirmities of ye Eyes especially such as are troubled with Inflammations but to Clear ye sight and Strengthen it and Preserve it Especialy of old women for yt reason its called break spectacles water for they yt use it need no spectacles, some few drops into ye eye morning and evening.[147]

Gerarde had obviously heard of this use of the 'blew-bottle or cornfloure' as he says 'some have thought the common Blew-Bottle to be of temperature something cold, and therefore good against the inflammation of the eyes, as some thinke'.[148]

John Pechey, in his herbal written some sixty years later says of blue-bottles,

> It grows commonly among corn. The Flowers and the distill'd Water are useful for Inflammations of the Eyes, and for the Blearedness of them.[149]

Presumably they must have been effective for their use to have persisted all this time. Now, alas, it would be difficult or impossible to gather wild cornflowers in East Anglia.

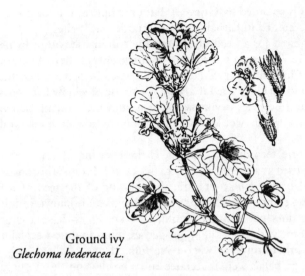

Ground ivy
Glechoma hederacea L.

Headache

Taylor collected several plant remedies for headache, as well as the vinegar bandage of Jack-and-Jill fame. His plant remedies include,

Smell horse radish. (Heydon, Norfolk)

Bind a cabbage leaf to the forehead. (Eyke WI, Suffolk)

Red roses, about half a gallon strong vinegar. Leave in close vessel for about a fortnight, then strain off the liquid – this is used as an embrocation for headaches. (Huntingfield WI, Suffolk)

This pleasant-sounding remedy is reminiscent of Gerarde:

The distilled water of roses is good for the strengthening of the heart and refreshing of the spirits.[150]

while Pechey tells us:

The Red Rose is astringent and bitter . . . A Decoction of it is used for the Head-ach.[151]

A wide variety of plant remedies for headache were recorded in the 1990s in East Anglia. Both dock leaves,[152] and rhubarb leaves[153] were used as a cooling application to the forehead, rather like the cabbage leaf recorded by Taylor. An infusion of lime tree flowers was used,[154] a remedy still favoured today in France.

Another pleasant remedy was an infusion of honeysuckle flowers.[155] This use

39

of honeysuckle flowers is recorded by Grieve,[156] but does not seem to be one of the uses for this plant recorded in herbals such as Gerarde and Pechey.

Willow bark was chewed for a headache, a remedy still in use within living memory in Lincolnshire. One man remembers his uncle always chewed willow bark for a hangover; he himself was given it as a child when he had a headache, but it made him sick and he never tried it again![157] The use of willow bark goes back at least to Biblical times (e.g. Leviticus 23). It is known to contain salicin in various forms, a fact which would certainly justify its use in fevers and pain.[158]

Another hangover cure recorded in Norfolk is the chewing of celery,[159] a plant more commonly used as a rheumatism cure (see p. 46). From Whissonsett in Norfolk comes yet another hangover cure: the chewing of the seed of the 'headache flower', as the common field poppy (*Papaver rhoeas*) is known in this county.[160] Although it does not contain opium, it is known to have a large number of alkaloids, some with pain-killing properties. This doubtless explains its use by the Land Girls during the war in Norfolk. If one of them had a fractious baby, red poppy petals were macerated in its bottle, and this ensured that the mother could work while the baby slept peacefully.[161]

The use of feverfew for headaches and migraine was recorded from four Norfolk schools, and from two individuals in Suffolk. This remedy has recently received a lot of publicity, since clinical trials in London showed its efficacy in migraine.[162] It is not clear whether these records of its use reflect a traditional use for the plant, or the modern resurgence of interest in its use. This point is discussed further in Chapter V.

A fascinating pain-killing remedy was recorded in 1900 from Essex:

> Thorn apple was used as a pain reliever. The top of the fruit was cut off, the inside pulped, and vinegar added. Inhalation of the fumes brought relief.[163]

The thorn apple (*Datura stramonium*) occurs throughout England as a natu-ralised weed in gardens. We have seen how it was used in the treatment of burns (see p. 23). It was also used, in the form of tobacco from the dried leaves, for the treatment of asthma, a use recorded in 1990 in Norfolk (see Appendix), and which, according to Grieve, was a practice introduced by Baron Storch in the latter half of the eighteenth century.[164] It has strongly narcotic as well as pain-killing properties. This Essex use for the plant has not so far been found elsewhere.

Kidney Complaints

The use of Yew twigs steeped in tea for kidney complaints was recorded in Lincolnshire in the 1920s (see Appendix). This seems a strange use for a tree known to be very poisonous. Fatalities among horses and cattle have often been

Twitch
Agropyron repens
(L.)Beauv.

recorded as a result of eating yew. Yet in some parts of Norfolk people remember playing a childhood game, a bit like Russian roulette, which consisted of eating the fleshy red aril of the yew berry and spitting out the seed. It was thought that death would result if the seed were swallowed. Evidently it was of great importance not to be discovered by parents to be playing this game, an added element of danger that doubtless added to its attraction.[165]

The yew is currently the subject of a clinical trial for its anti-cancer properties, and is showing very promising results, especially in the treatment of ovarian cancer.[166]

Kidney complaints, and more particularly cystitis, were treated in recent times in Norfolk by an infusion of the rhizomes of couch grass, known in the country as 'foul grass' or 'twitch' (*Agropyron repens*).[167] There were three records of this use from Norfolk and one from Essex. Interestingly, the plant has been shown to have 'broad antibiotic properties'.[168]

For urinary incontinence:

A concoction of plantine leaves is a sure cure if drunk night and morning.[169]

Which species of plantain was used is not absolutely clear, but it may well have been the common plantain (*Plantago major*), said by Grieve to have been 'good in disorders of the kidney'.[170] It is widely used in Chinese medicine for treating urinary disease.[171]

Jaundice

Taylor recorded an interesting collection of jaundice remedies in the 1920s:

> Take the pith of the barberry bush (*Berberis*) and boil it until there is a
> yellow liquid like tea. Give the patient a supful every day, and see that all
> the other food is yellow too. (This remedy was tried on us all as children,
> when we had jaundice through the house, by an old woman, Mrs Heyhoe,
> the then Vicar's housekeeper. We rather liked it as custards were included in
> the regimen and the 'tea' was not too bad when sweetened.)[172]

This is an interesting example of 'like curing like', the yellow children being
given yellow drink and yellow food! The plant is still used in the treatment of
jaundice and gall-stones.[173] It has a very large number of medicinally-active
ingredients.[174]

From Bocking Essex comes this remedy for jaundice: 'the bark of the spindle-
wood tree made with tea'.[175] Grieve records that this plant, *Euonymus atropur-
pureus*, is of particular value in liver diseases 'which follow or accompany
fever'.[176] The plant appears in the 1983 *British Herbal Pharmacopoeia*,[177] where,
among its other uses, it is listed as valuable in gall-bladder disease.

The use of hemp seed for jaundice was recorded by Huntingfield WI
(Suffolk) in the 1920s. Presumably, this refers to *Cannabis sativa*, the Indian
hemp. It doubtless made the sufferer feel better, even if it did not cure his
jaundice!

More soberly, dandelion tea was recommended by Earsham WI (Norfolk).
This has traditionally been regarded as good for the liver for many centuries.
Pechey (1694) describes it as 'epatick'.[178]

From Huntingfield in Suffolk comes the following recipe:

> Take a few leaves of celandine and boil in a pint of water, and when cold
> use as a drink, a wineglassful once a day.   (Huntingfield WI)

This probably refers to the greater celandine, *Chelidonium majus*, of which
Pechey writes in 1694, 'A syrup made of the whole Herb is good in the
jaundice'. Its use is still recommended in gall-bladder disease.[179]

The only plant remedy recorded in 1990 for jaundice was a decoction of
agrimony (*Agrimonia eupatoria*)[180] (see Appendix). Dioscorides described this
plant as 'a remedy for them that have bad livers', a reputation which has
survived into the twentieth century.[181]

Measles

Taylor collected three recommendations for measles: hot beer to 'bring the spots
out';[182] saffron tea[183] and marigold tea made as follows:

> 1 oz heads of marigolds in full flower, 1 pint boiling water. Let it stand.

Give to child in wineglass three times a day (warm). (Yoxford WI, Suffolk)

Saffron tea was much used for fevers in children as a diaphoretic (i.e. it induced sweating and therefore cooled down the patient). It was made from the dried stigmas of *Crocus sativa*, which was at one time grown commercially in East Anglia. A lady now living in Braintree, Essex, recalls her mother growing and drying saffron.[184]

One of the measles remedies collected in the 1990s interestingly combines two of Taylor's remedies:

For measles, an infusion of marigold blossoms was made and drunk, followed by a draught of hot old ale.[185]

For measles, fevers and 'flu', one lady living in Kenninghall recommends the use of yarrow tea (*Achillea millefolium*).[186] The known active constituents of yarrow are very numerous, and 'it is used for many complaints, throughout the world, with justification.[187]

For treating the sore eyes that accompany measles, one lady now living in Norwich remembers her mother using an infusion of the flowers of lesser celandine (*Ranunculus ficaria*).[188] This plant, as its common name of pilewort implies, is far better known for its use in treating haemorrhoids: in fact the author has been unable to find any reference to the use of the flowers in the way described above. The informant, herself botanically knowledgeable, is in no doubt about the identity of the plant used.

Piles

The famous pilewort (*Ranunculus ficaria*) is the only plant remedy recorded by Taylor for piles (Mr W., Mattishall, Norfolk).

Various plant recommendations have been made in the 1990s. An ointment made from garlic was used, with only limited success, by a lady in North Norfolk.[189]

Some interesting piles remedies come from an informant in Essex:

To cure piles, boil scabious in water, then let the patient sit over the steam. The herb pilewort applied in an ointment will help.

also

Take a large handful of red nettles, and infuse in a quart of white wine, in a jug, on a hot hearth, for one hour, take a wineglass full two or three times a day.[190]

The scabious (*Knautia arvensis*), has been used in a wide variety of ways since its recommendation by Culpeper and others, but no precedent has been found

Red nettle
Lamium purpureum L.

for this particular use. The red nettle is, presumably, *Lamium purpureum*, for which Grieve records various uses, particularly in staunching bleeding,[191] but again no record of its use in piles has been found. Although no printed record for the use of red nettles in piles has been found, it is interesting to compare this remedy with one appearing in an early eighteenth century Norfolk hand-written manuscript 'For the Coming Down of the Fundament':

> Take a quart of white wine, a handfull of redd nettles, chop them and boyle them . . . give it to the party to drink fasting . . . keep the herbs cleane and heat them and lay them on a cloth and put up the place greeved with them.[192]

The use of pilewort ointment is also recorded by this same informant.

Another Essex resident, who spent much of his life in High Easter, has this information concerning piles:

> One day while talking to an elderly lady she pulled out an handkerchief from her pocket and in so doing brought out with it several large rose hips. I gathered up the rose hips and in returning them to her inquired 'to what purpose she carried them?' Do you really want to know?' she replied. She then related that if you carried rose hips on you it would prevent you having piles. The same lady also carried in her pocket a small potato which was almost black with age and petrified – this was a certain cure for rheumatism.
>
> Another treatment for piles related to me by an old man was to go out in the early morning and bath them in fresh dew – this is not really very much different than the treatment used sometimes today of iced water.

One day in Pleshey I encountered a man coming along the Back Lane with some pieces of ground elder (*Aegopodium podagraria*) in his weeding basket. 'That's a terrible useless plant, Fred', I remarked – 'serves no useful purpose I know of!' Fred then told me, 'I only know one thing it is good for and that is to boil some of it up, and then, when cold, use the solution on piles – it will cure them'.[193]

This use of ground elder, a plant renowned by Culpeper and Gerarde for its effect on gout, has not been found elsewhere.

Where a plant remedy involves simply carrying the plant, as in the case of the rose-hips, above, it is tempting to speculate that such a custom represents a vestige of an earlier use of the plant as a medicine. Roses were used as a constituent of many medicines, including gargles,[194] but so far no record of the use of hips in pile treatment has been found. This idea will be discussed further when remedies for rheumatism are considered (p. 46).

Rheumatism, Sciatica, Lumbago, Back Pain, Arthritis

The Norfolk King of the Poachers, Rolf, summed up the situation when he wrote:

> My grandmother had a cure of sorts for evrything, and herbs for evry complaint . . . all could be cured some way or another except the rhumatics, and I think that is incurable.[195]

However, this did not deter East Anglians in the early years of this century from using plants to alleviate the suffering caused by rheumtism in all its forms. Here is the information collected by Taylor in the 1920s:

> Belladonna is used for embrocations.   (E.H., Ingham, Norfolk)

> A decoction of the seed of buckbean is used for rheumatism.   (M.B.)

> Two or three drops of oil of juniper on a lump of sugar every morning. (S.B., Norwich).

> Boil an ounce of celery seed in a pint of water until reduced to half a pint. Strain. Bottle and cork carefully. Take one teaspoonful twice a day in a little water. (Cringleford WI, Norfolk)

> Bryony root, which can be dug up in gardens, or growing wild, makes a good liniment if washed and boiled a good long time, and the liquor used as a liniment or for a compress. (Ashby WI, Norfolk)

> Marshmallow sweets for cure of ague and rheumatism. (Dr R., Boston, Lincs.).

> Clover water – remedy for rheumatism.   (Huntingfield WI, Suffolk)

A large number of rheumatic remedies were collected in the 1990s, some of them the same as those collected by Taylor. Belladonna plasters are still available commercially, and occasionally used to relieve the pain of lumbago. Juniper oil is likewise still recommended.[196] An infusion of celery seeds is still in use for rheumatism.[197] Bryony root and clover water both figure in recently collected remedies, but not for rheumatism (see Appendix).

Among other recently-collected remedies for rheumatic complaints are the following:

> Wormwood, agrimony, and chicory, dried and infused for lumbago and rheumatism.[198]
>
> Yarrow roots infused as a drink for rheumatism.[199]
>
> Angelica 'was used for rheumatics'.[200]
>
> Willow bark was chewed for arthritis and 'seaweed' was used for rheumatism.[201]
>
> Sea lettuce was stewed in sea water and applied as a poultice to ease the pain of bunions and arthritis in the feet. Bladder-wrack was also used: hot water was run on the bladder-wrack in the bath, and the resulting slime released from the bladders eased the pain of arthritis.[202]
>
> Eating parsley is considered good for arthritis.[203]
>
> One Norfolk man in his nineties reckons to have cured himself of the pain of arthritis simply by eating parsley every day for a year.[204]
>
> Horse-radish root, grated and made into a poultice was used to relieve lumbago.[205]
>
> To relieve lumbago, first apply heat to relieve the pain, and loose the muscles, then apply a poultice made from hot linseed, hot nettle leaves.[206]
>
> A tea made from stinging nettles is recommended for sciatica,[207] and also for arthritis.[208]

A lady now living in Essex, but brought up on the Romney Marsh, recalls various childhood remedies:

> I think my favourite is the one written in her own handwriting in my mother's old recipe book – for cabbage water:
> Boil the outside leaves of a cabbage in water till tender then strain. Drink half a cup of this each day. A sure cure for rheumatism – WITH FAITH.[209]

An infusion of strawberry leaves or roots was used as a drink for rheumatism.[210] Linnaeus used the berries for treating gout.[211] Alternatively, oak bark could be boiled, and the resulting liquor drunk for rheumatism.[212]

Interestingly enough, there is one record of an acorn being carried in the pocket to ward off rheumatism.[213] This could lend support to the idea mentioned above that the custom of carrying a plant to ward off an illness could relate to an earlier use of the same plant in a remedy.

There are several records of a potato being carried in this way, to ward off rheumatism.[214] Although no rheumatism remedy involving potatoes has been recorded so far for East Anglia, there is a record of their use in eighteenth-century Scotland, where bathing the feet in the water in which potatoes had been cooked 'as hot as can be borne' was regarded as a remedy for rheumatism.[215]

Grieve refers to the tradition of carrying a potato to ward off rheumatism and refers to 'experiments in the treatment of rheumatism and gout (which) have in the last few years been made with preparations of raw potato juice . . . the acute pain is much relieved by fomentations of the prepared juice'. She also refers to the use of hot potato water.[216]

Of the other plants used in the treatment of rheumatism, and recorded by Taylor and by the present author, many are mentioned by Grieve as being useful for rheumatic complaints, e.g. belladonna (from *Atropa belladonna*), buckbean or bogbean (*Menyanthes trifoliata*), celery (*Apium graveolens*), bryony root (*Bryonia dioica*), wormwood (*Artemisia sp*), yarrow (said by Grieve to be used in Norway for the treatment of rheumatism, p. 864) (*Achillea millefolium*), Angelica (*Angelica archangelica*), bladderwrack (*Fucus vesiculosis*), strawberry (*Fragaria vesca*). However, no similar uses are recorded by Grieve for the following plants: chicory (*Cichorium intybus*), clover (*Trifolium sp*), agrimony (*Agrimonia eupatoria*), willow (*Salix sp*), sea lettuce, parsley (*Carum petroselinum*), stinging nettle (*Urtica dioica*), cabbage (*Brassica sp*) and oak (*Quercus robur*).

Another plant sometimes carried to ward off rheumatism is the nutmeg (*Myristica fragrans*).[217]. It is interesting to note that this plant has now been shown to contain a prostaglandin inhibitor[218] which would explain its use in anti-rheumatic liniments. No record has been found of its use in domestic medicine in this way, but the carrying of a nutmeg may represent all that is left of such a practice.

From Mundford Primary School in Norfolk comes a record (1980) of the wearing of a necklace of conkers to ward off rheumatism. This, again, could be a 'residual' use of a plant formerly used medicinally. Grieve records that,

> the fruits (of horse chestnut) have been employed in the treatment of rheumatism and neuralgia'. (p. 193)

When discussing the treatment of gout with ground elder (*Aegopodium padagraria*), Culpeper states that

> It is not to be supposed Goutwort hath its name for nothing, but upon experiment to heal the gout and sciatica: as also joint aches and other cold griefs. The very bearing of it about one eases the pains of the gout and defends him that bears it from the disease. (Grieve, p. 369)

So obviously the idea of wearing as well as eating medicinal plants is not a new one!

Lastly, there are several records for the use of feverfew (*Chrysanthemum parthenium*) for arthritis (e.g. Denton & Alburgh School, Norfolk; Docking School, Norfolk). However, it is not clear whether these represent 'secondary' knowledge of plant uses, following the publicity surrounding clinical studies of feverfew for arthritis and migraine. This point will be discussed further in Chapter V.

SKIN CONDITIONS

Under this broad heading will be considered plant remedies for a wide variety of ailments.

Bites and Stings

Here are the remedies that Taylor recorded in the 1920s:

> House leek – or houseliek as it is commonly called is very good to allay irritation – bruise the fleshy leaves and apply the juice – sometimes it is mixed with cream (in case of vaccination or insect bites or rash).[219]

> Nettle stings – juice from its stalk. I am told this is a fact.[220]

In the 1990s, two other remedies were recorded: first, tobacco, well-chewed and then rubbed onto bites and stings;[221] secondly, raw onion rubbed onto bites and stings (numerous records, see Appendix). The houseleek (*Sempervivum tectorum*), as we shall see, was used for a wide variety of skin conditions. The use of nettle-stalk juice to soothe the sting of nettle is recommended in John Wesley's Primitive Physick. John Pechey in his *Compleat Herbal* (1694) tells us 'Juice of Nettles, cures the Stings of Nettles presently'.[222] So this home remedy has certainly been in use for some time!

Interestingly, the use of chewed tobacco on stings appears in the manuscript *Gunton Household Book*, among the early eighteenth century remedies.[223]

Cracked and Chapped Skin

The papery outer skin of an onion laid on a cracked lip will heal it, we are told by Bealings WI, Norfolk (recorded by Taylor, 1920). From North Norfolk in the 1990s comes the suggestion of an ointment made from 'samphire' for healing cracked skin. This is the marsh samphire, *Salicornia*, still eaten in many parts of Norfolk as a vegetable.[224] A man now living in Lowestoft but brought up near Holt in Norfolk vividly remembers suffering with badly chapped legs in the winter. A horseman advised him to wrap large dock leaves round his legs, and tie them in place under his trousers. This brought great relief.[225]

The juice of houseleeks was recommended for chapped lips.[226]

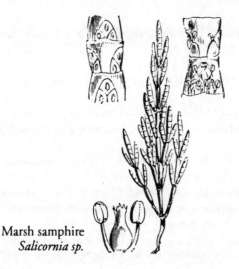

Marsh samphire
Salicornia sp.

An ointment made from the flowers of the elder (*Sambucus nigra*) was soothing for rough hands.[227]

The use of elderflowers and of houseleek in numerous skin complaints is well-recorded, but the use of samphire and of dock leaves for chapped skin has not been found in print.

Dermatitis and Rashes

In the 1920s, Taylor recorded the drinking of nettle tea as a cure for nettle-rash (Dr R.G., and Eyke WI, Suffolk). This same remedy was recorded from Essex in 1990, from a lady now living in Colchester, but brought up in Kent:

> Living as a child in the middle of the Romney Marsh in Kent, where the only means of transport were a bicycle or walking, and the nearest doctor four-and-a-half miles away, each family had its own 'patent medicines'. When we needed help, we naturally went to my Gran, who would not only cure us, but was also the area midwife. She had helped to deliver over 250 babies before the law in 1936 said only registered midwives could deliver babies . . . Other herbal cures were nettle tea, made by boiling the heads of stinging nettles, then straining and drinking the water. This was very tasty with sugar and was a very good cure for a rash.[228]

A severe case of dermatitis which had failed to yield to hospital treatment was successfully cured in the 1950s by using a poultice made from lightly boiled chickweed shoots (*Stellaria media*). This remedy has been passed on to several other people who have also used it with success.[229] The juice from stonecrop

(*Sedum acre*) has also been used in relatively recent (1950s) time to treat dermatitis.[230]

An interesting remedy for dermatitis, which became locally famous, was recommended by a man then living in Ingham, Norfolk. Again, the patient had had unsuccessful treatment from the hospital. She was advised to gather the roots of the marsh dock ('take the plants that grow with their feet in the water') and boil them and use the resulting liquid to bathe the rash. She used it with such success that in subsequent years she always made up a bottle of this, which was used for treating any rash, sunburn, etc., and was lent to neighbours with great success.[231]

The marsh dock (*Rumex palustris*) is a relatively uncommon plant, but does occur in 'the old fenland peat of south-west Norfolk',[232] so it is possible, though hard to prove, that the docks gathered from Ingham in the 1940s were indeed true marsh docks. Most of the marsh in the vicinity of the house where the patient then lived has now been drained.

Other remedies recorded specifically for the treatment of sunburn include an infusion of meadowsweet,[233] the water in which sage has been boiled,[234] and an infusion of the leaves of vervain.[235] This last remedy is an example of information that has only just survived. The informant, now in her seventies, was brought up by an aunt who 'knew the use of every plant growing on the common'; as a little girl, she remembers her aunt using all kinds of plants for all kinds of ailments, but this use of vervain leaves is one of the few she recalls with certainty.

Of the plants described here for use in dermatitis and rashes, only chickweed (*Stellaria media*) is described in this context by Grieve[236] and others. Although the other plants have all been used medicinally, this specific use has not been found in print for marsh dock (*Rumex palustris*), meadowsweet (*Filipendula ulmaria*), sage (*Salvia officinalis*), stonecrop (*Sedum acre*) or vervain (*Verbena officinalis*).

Eczema

Taylor in the 1920s recorded four plant remedies for eczema. The first comes from Cringleford WI, Norfolk:

Boil a bunch of elderberry shoots and use the liquid.

Huntingfield WI, Suffolk, have this suggestion:

Take a few sprays of rue, boil them for five minutes and when cool bathe the inflammation of the skin with the liquid and poultice with a few of the leave on parts that burn and tingle and itch.

The last two remedies come from an informant in Bocking, Essex:

Squeeze out juice from some houseleeks and mix with cream. Apply as

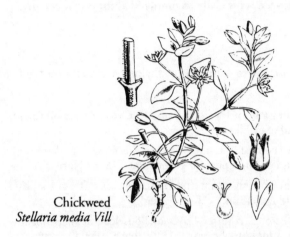

Chickweed
Stellaria media Vill

ointment. Sure cure in about 7–10 days. Dock root boiled and mixed with lard also a good remedy.

These two were also recommended for treating shingles.

Elder was still in use for the treatment of eczema in Norfolk in the 1960s. It was used in two ways: either an infusion of the flowers was used to bathe the affected parts, or the fresh green leaves were rubbed directly onto the skin. These methods have been used with success both on horse and man.[237]

Chickweed poultices, as described under dermatitis, have also been used with success in treating children with eczema.[238] An infusion of dandelion leaves, used to bathe the affected areas, was recommended by a lady now living near Norwich.[239]

A man now living in Lowestoft, but brought up near Holt in Norfolk, vividly described how his little brother suffered as a child from eczema. It was making everyone's lives miserable as the child was unable to sleep at night. A friend suggested to his mother that she should visit an old lady at Wiveton who know how to cure it. This his mother did, and returned with a jar of ointment which dramatically improved the child's eczema, and the quality of family life. The mother returned to Wiveton to thank the old lady and ask what was in the ointment. She was told it was simply houseleek juice mixed with single cream. Thereafter the family made up their own supply, and used it whenever it was needed. Years later, the older brother recalled this remedy when he heard of a friend of his granddaughter, a hairdresser by profession, who was very troubled by eczema on her hands. He told the girl about houseleek juice, and it worked wonders, and 'Now I've got a friend for life!'[240]

Although enjoying a widespread fame for its use in skin conditions generally, the specific use of houseleek for eczema does not seem to appear in herbal literature, nor does the use described above of elder flowers and leaves, or of dandelion leaves. Chickweed is officially recommended for use in eczema.[241]

Sores and Ulcers

A variety of plant remedies were collected by Taylor for the treatment of sores and ulcers:

> Clean ivy leaves – dressing for ulcers and sore feet: elderflower ointment. (Dr T., Oulton Broad, Norfolk)

> Green leaves of celery cooked in home dried lard (to make sure there is no salt in it) strained, and put into pots for general use. (S.B., Norwich)

> Take equal quantities of fresh cream and houseleek juice (from the leaf) then apply to the sore as a cream. (Huntingfield WI, Suffolk)

> St John's wort for bedsores; comfrey leaves or houseleek or marshmallow for inflammation as a local application. (The above were all communicated to me by a very shrewd old monthly nurse – Dr W.H.B., Lincoln)

> Leaf of plantain for sores and cuts. (Mrs M. Wivenhoe, Essex)

Among the recently-collected plant remedies for sores and ulcers, houseleek again appears,[242] as does an ointment made from the inner bark, leaves and flowers of elder,[243] and an ointment made from the crushed seeds of marshmallow in lard.[244] A rotten apple is recommended as a rub for 'any sore place':[245] this is an interesting use of moulds before antibiotics were officially used. The informant, who used this as a child, is now in his seventies. Solomon's seal was made into an ointment for treating ulcers and wounds in horses and cattle.[246] The leaves and flowers of lesser celandine, heated in lard, made an ointment, again recommended 'for any sore place'.[247] Hedge garlic leaves (*Alliaria petiolata*) were chewed as a cure for mouth ulcers.[248] Leg ulcers were treated with the bruised leaves of broad-leaved plantain (*Plantago major*);[249] or with cabbage leaves;[250] or an ointment made from comfrey root;[251] or ivy leaves laid on.[252]

Although various medicinal uses for all these plants are recorded in the literature, the specific uses cited above for sores and ulcers are not documented, with the exception of hedge garlic.[253]

Spots, Pimples and Corns

Taylor in the 1920s recorded several remedies for corns, most involving ivy leaves:

> Bind an ivy leave on the corn. (D.R.G., Debenham, Suffolk)

> Soak some tender ivy leaves in strong vinegar for some days, then grind in a

Vervain
Verbena officinalis L.

mortar to a paste, and paint the corn with it.   (S.B., Norwich, but an Essex remedy)

An ivy leaf grown on an ash tree is a certain cure for a corn.   (Earsham WI, Norfolk)

The last remedy involves a different plant, the unrelated ground ivy (*Glechoma hederacea*):

Take a leaf of ground ivy, rub with pure lard. Tie on the corn and leave for three days, when it can be turned out. (Wilby WI, Suffolk)

Corn cures recorded from the 1980s again include ivy: the leaf is bruised and stuck on the corn like a corn plaster.[254] Willow bark ground in vinegar was also recommended.[255] This latter treatment is of interest in that willow bark contains salicylates, still an official component of many corn plasters.

An infusion of elderflowers was claimed to 'fade freckles'.[256] Compare this with Grieve's comment:

Elderflower water in our great-grandmother's days was a household word for clearing the complexion of freckles and sunburn, and keeping it in a good condition.[257]

Drinking nettle tea is claimed to 'clear pimples'.[258] For spots, and in particular for the spots of impetigo, the juice from marigold leaves has been found useful.[259] Finally, from Wicklewood in Norfolk comes this recipe which made its designer, 'Billy' locally celebrated:

Oak apples steeped in strong wine and vinegar with flowers of sulphur and a decoction of root of iris removed freckles, spots and cured many skin complaints.[260]

Although many of the plants described here appear in the herbalist literature as used for skin complaints, the specific uses described here are not documented. Gerarde describes the use of iris root in removing bruise marks,[261] but it would seem that this recipe is Billy's own invention.

Stomach Pain and Indigestion

Dandelion tea was recommended in 1920 by Wilby WI, to treat indigestion. In the 1990s, several remedies for indigestion in animals were collected. These include: shoots of rose fed to goats for indigestion;[262] comfrey leaves were used in the same way for horses, chickens and geese;[263] ivy leaves fed to sheep could cure digestive problems – 'If a sheep won't eat ivy you may as well give up on it';[264] an infusion of houseleek was used to cure human stomach ache,[265] as was an infusion of mint, mixed with ginger;[266] oil of wheat was recommended for 'gastritis'.[267] One lady has very vivid memories of being dosed with 'herbygrass' (rue, or herb of grace, *Ruta graveolens*) for stomach ache. She remembers the disgustingly bitter taste, and also the repulsive appearance of the infusion as it 'matured'. Perhaps part of its effectiveness was as a deterrent – one would only complain of stomach ache in that household if the pain was really bad![268] Grieve mentions rue as, among other properties, a 'mild stomachic'.[269] Culpeper claimed that rose leaves, externally applied 'strengthen a weak stomach'.[270] Otherwise, no exact precedents have been found for these East Anglian stomach remedies.

Teething and Toothache

Taylor gathered a wide variety of interesting plant remedies for toothache:

> Putting the kernel of an onion in the cavity of the tooth. (Dr N., Huntingdon)
>
> Tying feverfew on wrist for toothache on opposite side. (Dr J.H.M.B., Wrentham, Suffolk)
>
> If tooth aches the right side of the face, grate horseradish and put it on the left wrist for twenty minutes. Place it on the right wrist for same length of time if left side of face aches. (Surlingham WI, Norfolk)
>
> Cabbage leaves applied as poultices for toothache. (Miss G., Attleborough, Norfolk)
>
> Poultice of feverfew. (Orford WI, Suffolk)
>
> Smoke from burned senna leaves inhaled. (Sproughton WI, Suffolk).

In the 1990s the following plant remedies for toothache were collected: to ease teething in infants, they were sometimes given a dummy dipped in poppy seeds;[271] another remedy was to soften the leaves of groundsel in their milk,[272] or to use figwort, 'bruff betony'.[273] The use of this plant for toothache is mentioned by Grieve.[274]

For older sufferers, henbane root soaked in vinegar was used,[275] or bramble leaves could be chewed;[276] this was a remedy of gipsy origin. There were numerous records of chewing a clove for toothache, a practice still widely used today, or applying clove oil on cotton wool. Finally, the juice from bistort leaves was rubbed round horses teeth to prevent decay.[277] Interestingly, this plant, *Polygonum bistorta* is still recommended as a mouthwash in modern day herbalism.[278] Henbane, *Hyoscyamus niger*, is a well-known sedative and pain-killer, with properties much like those of belladonna, but again this specific use of the plant has not been found in the current herbal literature. The same applies to other toothache remedies (interestingly, both horse-radish and cabbage leaves were recorded by Newman and Wilson as home-cures for toothache in Essex, recorded 1951).[279]

The use of henbane for toothache certainly goes back a long way, as this comment in Tippermalloch's *Poor Man's Physician* (1731) shows:

> Worms of the teeth are cured with the smoke of henbane-seed put upon hot coals, and received through a tunnel, and that miraculously.[280]

Gerarde, writing a century earlier, was more cynical:

> The root (of henbane) boiled with vinegre, & the same holden hot on the mouth, easeth the pain of the teeth. The seed is used by Mountibank tooth-drawers which run about the country, to cause worms come forth of the teeth, by burning it in a chafing dish of coles, the party holding his mouth over the fume thereof; but some craft companions to gain mony convey small lute-strings into the water, persuading the patient, that those small creepers came out of his mouth or other parts which he intended to ease.[281]

Tonics

The concept of a 'spring-time tonic' is now an old-fashioned one; it was felt to be a good idea to 'purify the blood' after the winter, and the various brews used to achieve this have lingered in the minds of the people who were given them; some pleasant memories, others decidedly unpleasant.

Taylor recorded a spring-time tonic composed of:

> Haryhound with dandelions and blackcurrant. (Miss G., Attleborough, Norfolk)

Haryhound is a country name for horehound (*Marrubium vulgare*) which was made into horehound beer in many country homes in East Anglia in the early part of this century.

Henbane
Hyoscyamus niger L.

In the 1980s and 1990s, the following 'tonics' have been recorded:

Horse-pepper (wild angelica). Young shoots eaten in spring time as a tonic.[282]

Elderberry wine 'as a tonic'; rue 'tea' as a spring tonic; comfrey tea 'as a tonic and good for the blood'.[283]

Dock leaves 'chewed as a tonic'.[284]

Nettles in various forms were regarded as a good spring-time tonic. Sometimes they were made into 'nettle puddings' with lemon juice and egg white.[285] Another version was to make them into beer, sometimes combined with goosegrass (*Galium aparine*):

To keep blood clear, in the early summer my grandmother would brew up what was called 'nettle beer'. This consisted of nettles and cleavers or goosegrass (*Galium aparine*) which with possibly some ground ginger were covered in boiling water and steeped for several days. It was then strained and some yeast and sugar added to work it for a few days. The result was a pleasant, slightly fizzy drink which my brother and I enjoyed drinking.[286]

This was presumably an Essex equivalent of the dandelion and burdock drink popular in the north of England, and still available commercially.

Warts

As a retired Norfolk schoolteacher pointed out,[287] warts and their treatment really need a book to themselves! The present author, as a botanist, has been

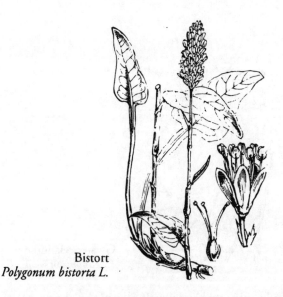

Bistort
Polygonum bistorta L.

primarily concerned with the recording of plant remedies, but has incidentally come across a number of 'charms' and superstitions surrounding many complaints, as well as household remedies not containing plant ingredients. It is hoped that these will form the subject of a separate volume.

For the other complaints discussed in this chapter, it seems possible to build up a reasonable picture of their home treatment, simply from plant remedies alone. With warts, however, it is a different matter. Everyone who recalls the treatment of warts in earlier days remembers 'magical' ways of getting rid of them, either at the hands of a 'wart-charmer', or by following a recognised ceremony such as the rubbing on of (preferably stolen) meat, followed by its burial. As the meat decays, so will the wart.

Taylor, working in the 1920s, was interested in 'animal charm-cures' as well as plant remedies, and many of these are included among his manuscript notes. The plant remedies collected both by Taylor and by the present author represent then, not the entire picture of home treatment of warts, but merely one aspect of it. This seems to be far more true for warts than for any other ailment discussed. With this proviso in mind, let us look at the plant remedies used in East Anglia for the treatment of warts.

Taylor recorded the following plant remedies for warts:

Juice from milkweed or milk thistle (Stamford School).
Juice from stem of a spurge (Dr, Huntingdon).
Juice of greater celandine (Mrs B., Norwich) also Wilby WI, Suffolk.
Juice of milkwort (two records, Lincolnshire and Suffolk).
Juice of hogweed and ground elder both cure warts (Tacolneston WI);
    broad bean pod rubbed on (two records, Norwich).

Greater celandine
Chelidonium majus L.

'Take a lemon and cut in halfs, rubbing juice from same on the warts as often as possible until seeds form. And can then be taken out by the roots, which is quite painless' (Wilby WI, Suffolk).

The plant remedies for warts collected in the past ten years include:

    Milkweed juice[288]
    Sun spurge juice[289]
    Greater celandine juice[290]
    Sloe berry rubbed on[291]
    Juice of a fig leaf[292]
    Dandelion juice[293]
    Juice from the stalk of crowfoot dropped on[294]
    Houseleek rubbed on[295]

It is of interest that 'juice of spurge', 'juice of the greater celandine' and the 'root of crowfoot bruised' all appear among Moncrief's recommendations for warts in 1731.[296] In more modern times, several of these plants are recommended by Grieve for treating warts, e.g., 'The milky juice of the freshly-broken stalk of a fig has been found to remove warts on the body.'[297] Dandelion, greater celandine, crowfoot (*Ranunculus acris*), houseleek, spurges, are all mentioned in connection with the treatment of warts in domestic medicine.

All the plant remedies collected by Taylor in the 1920s and by the present author during the past ten years, are summarised in the Appendix. Where possible, the approximate date of birth of the informant is given. It will be seen that a number of miscellaneous remedies for ailments other than those discussed in this chapter, have also been included. It seems important to record such information, since the generation of people with knowledge of domestic plant medicine in rural East Anglia has now reached their seventies. In the experience of the present author, such knowledge has never been written down, and in most cases has not been handed down orally either to the next generation. Sometimes people are afraid of being laughed at for their old-fashioned ideas. In other instances, they have not told younger people because they did not see such information as being of interest.

CHAPTER THREE

Sources of information

Dr Taylor's methods of collecting information
and those of the present author

THE LAST CHAPTER has presented a selection of the plant remedies collected by Dr Taylor in the 1920s and by the present author in the past few years. The methods by which this information has been amassed are of interest in themselves. The purpose of this chapter is to compare and contrast Dr Taylor's sources with those of the present study, undertaken in a similar area some seventy years later.

The first important point to make is that most of Dr Taylor's work relies on primary sources. Very little indeed is quoted from printed texts. This point has two-fold significance. In the first place, at least in the view of the present author, this means that it represents more accurately folk medicine as it was actually practised in East Anglia in the 1920s.

It is beyond the scope of the present work to give a detailed exposition of the reliability of oral evidence. George Ewart Evans in his book *Where Beards Wag All* points out:

> In my experience of recording the skills and crafts of the old rural culture I have found that the testimony of the craftsman is more accurate than the average printed source.[1]

This seems to be equally true in the field of domestic remedies. A story from the author's experience vividly illustrates this point.

Knowing of my interest in old remedies, a local farmer very kindly lent me a book in his possession called *Farriery Improved*, published in 1789. On page 68 we read:

> To provoke lust in mares.
> If you have any particular opportunity of a fine stallion when your mare is not naturally disposed to receive him, or will not stand to be covered: in this case, to provoke lust in her, give her drink of clarified honey and new milk mixed together; and then with a bunch of nettles pat her hinder-parts, and immediately after offer her the horse, which she will receive.[2]

Shortly after reading this, I was speaking to an old man in his nineties, who all his working days had led a shire horse stallion around the farms of Norfolk,

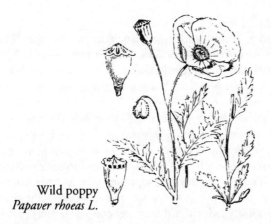

Wild poppy
Papaver rhoeas L.

sleeping rough at nights, often alongside the horse. In the course of conversation, I asked him whether he had come across this use of stinging nettles. He laughed until the tears ran down his weathered face. When he had recovered sufficiently to speak, he told me:

> They books, they get it all wrong! You beat the mare with the nettles *after* the stallion has been!

which does, of course, make a lot more physiological sense!.[3]

Here is another example where the books apparently get it wrong! In a book on folklore of the Broads, it is stated 'Wild poppies are called "headaches" and are never brought into houses; they are considered to bring ill-luck to the gatherer.' This plant is still known in some parts of Norfolk as the headache flower, Its seeds were chewed as a cure for hangover, which seems a more likely explanation of the name.[4]

These two examples serve to illustrate the value of obtaining information straight from the people who actually used it. Any error that once appears in print is liable to be reproduced and perpetuated.

Dr Taylor's work is very largely based on information gathered directly from people who used it, or from their doctors.

The other significant point about Taylor's use of primary sources is that, in the experience of the present author, the field of domestic plant remedies is one which relies primarily for its survival on word of mouth. Very few of these remedies were written down. Those that were tend to be copied from earlier printed works, and there is no way of knowing whether they were actually used. In contrast, the plant remedies described by country people were ones they themselves had experience of using.

The present author has also relied almost entirely on oral evidence in collecting East Anglian plant remedies, so from this point of view, the two bodies of data are comparable.

61

Sources used by Dr Mark Taylor

Taylor's two main sources of information were branches of the Women's Institute, and family doctors. In his notes, information from twenty different branches of the Women's Institute is recorded, and from sixteen family doctors in Norfolk, Suffolk and Lincolnshire. In addition, remedies obtained from nine individual non-medical informants is included.

It is interesting to speculate on the reactions of the family doctors to whom Dr Taylor wrote asking for information. As we have seen in Chapter 1, the family doctor in rural East Anglia probably did not number a large proportion of agricultural workers among his patients. He would tend to see the better-off among the population. It could therefore be supposed that any plant remedies which he heard of would be supplied by the less poor among his patients; in fact, by that sector of society which did not depend so heavily on home treatment in times of illness. Possibly then, one would expect to see some differences between the data supplied via the family doctor and that obtained from questioning local branches of the Women's Institute. This idea will be explored more fully in Chapter 4, after the remedies themselves have been described.

As to the accuracy of information obtained by Dr Taylor, this is obviously difficult to assess, especially in the case of remedies obtained via doctors, whose information would certainly have been second-hand, if not more remote from the original use of the remedy. It could be argued that data from the Women's Institute might be more reliable, simply because it was supplied by people who themselves used the remedies.

Relying on correspondence, as Dr Taylor seems largely to have done, would inevitably limit the sources of information. It is an effort to write a letter, more so than having a conversation.

In the author's own experience, many elderly people, when first asked about plant remedies, have denied any knowledge of them. However, if in the course of conversation, one asks about how minor ailments were dealt with in their childhood, all kinds of information emerges, often including plant remedies which were clearly regarded not as a subject in themselves, but as an accepted part of life.

The author has found local radio to be of enormous help in making contact with people with this kind of information. It is rather ironical that Dr Taylor, some seventy years ago, attempted to present a radio programme on the subject of folk medicine, and this was blocked by the officials in the Ministry of Health. Perhaps they felt that it was inappropriate for their first full-time regional Medical Officer to be associated with such a study? (see letter dated May 27, 1927, written by Dr Taylor to the BBC).[5]

As Dr Taylor himself put it, he had done no more than 'sunk a few trial shafts' in the question for information. He did not have the opportunity to follow these up. The present author has found that in many instances, people

TAYLOR 1920

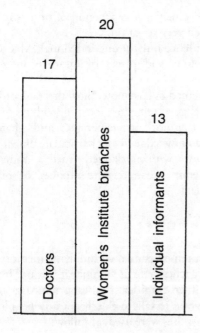

Analysis of sources of
information

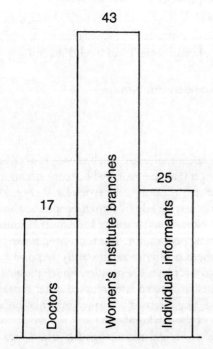

Numbers of plant remedies
provided by the sources

remember more and more about home remedies over a period of time, so that re-contacting such individuals has proved very rewarding.

Among Dr Taylor's notes there is evidence only of one individual (Mrs S.B. of Norwich) from whom repeated letters and pieces of information were received.

Others working in the field of plant remedies have noted how there are only a few individuals who have a wide knowledge of remedies: most individuals recall only one or two.[6] This, too, has been the author's own experience, and is hardly a surprising finding: experts with a wide knowledge of any particular subject are much thinner on the ground than those with a relatively small amount of knowledge. The accompanying histogram illustrates the number of plant remedies per informant in Dr Taylor's data.

Sources used by the present author

In the quest for information about plant remedies used within living memory in East Anglia, a number of different approaches were used. Since it was not book knowledge of herbal medicine, but rather empirical domestic remedies that were sought, the obvious line of enquiry was to talk to elderly country people in the area. To find these people, five approaches were used, as follows:

1. Requests for information via local radio and television.
2. Articles in local newspapers and magazines.
3. Chatting to people in village shops.
4. Enquiries to branches of the Women's Institute.
5. The giving of talks on the subject of plant remedies to local clubs and societies.

Each of these methods will now be considered in turn.

1. Local radio and television

Staff of both were extremely helpful. Local radio was much more productive of information than television, and it might be worthwhile considering the possible reasons for this. Probably the main reason is the type of audience: local radio stations are listened to during the day largely by retired people, so the age group was right for this study. Radio Norfolk has a strong bias towards country matters, so that it selects a rural listening population. The most productive type of programme was the phone-in, where people could instantly respond with information. It was then possible to contact later the people who telephoned.

Some of those who phoned in, when contacted later recalled other remedies in addition; others knew of only one single remedy. Further information was sometimes forthcoming from friends of those who phoned in.

Those individuals with memories of several plant remedies often recalled further examples over the next months, so that it proved very worthwhile to stay in touch with them. One man, now living in Lowestoft, told of a remedy for eczema. In subsequent letters and conversations he mentioned several other remedies, and over a period of two years has recalled seven plant remedies used in his youth.[7] A lady, now living in Norwich but brought up in the country, again phoned in with one remedy. When visited, she recalled eight more: over the subsequent eighteen months she has added five more remedies, as she has remembered them.[8]

Appeals for information on local television interestingly brought little by way of response; and no information at all was forthcoming after a local television programme included an account of the author's work. Presumably the main reason for this is that watching television is a purely passive affair; few people have pen and paper to hand, and few will bother to react.

2. *Local press*

Articles on local newspapers brought much more by way of response, though, per article appearing, this was still behind local radio as a source of information. The readers represent a wider, but possibly more town-based, section of society. Also, it is more trouble to write a letter than to phone a local radio station.

It is of interest that a short letter in the *Daily Mirror* some years ago brought in a flood of information from all over the country. This obviously reflects in part the far greater circulation of a national, as opposed to local, newspaper; it may also reflect a different type of reader.

3. *Village shops*

These were found to be a useful source of information. The owners, or customers, were often able to suggest elderly people in the area who might have the kind of country knowledge required. As with all the other sources used, a 'snowball' effect was found, one person suggesting others who suggested others.

4. *Branches of the Women's Institute*

The Women's Institute is a time-honoured source of information on country matters. However, in this particular case it has proved disappointing. Requests for information from members of local branches have brought in very little by way of authentic domestic country remedies. A vivid illustration of this is provided by one local branch. In the 1920s, Dr Mark Taylor contacted members of twenty-two branches of the Women's Institute. One particular branch supplied no fewer than fourteen different home remedies at one of their meetings held in 1925.[9] The author contacted the present secretary of the same Women's Institute branch who kindly agreed to request all members to report at a meeting any plant remedies that they remembered. Two remedies were presented at this meeting in 1991, one being the almost universally-known use of dock leaves for nettle stings.

So where has all the knowledge gone? One obvious answer is that, with the advent of the National Health Service, knowledge of country remedies has died out. However, this can only be a partial explanation, since a significant body of information on the subject has been gathered from other sources. It is the author's impression that the membership of the Women's Institute has changed dramatically during those intervening years. Many Norfolk villages have been overrun with incomers, and the local branches of the Women's Institute have been taken over largely by non-Norfolk people. It is noticeable at these meetings that it is sometimes difficult to find anyone who has been born and brought up in that particular area. This relative scarcity of local members probably explains the rather small amount of information obtained on domestic plant remedies.

5. *Talks given to other local societies and clubs*

This was not found to be a particularly productive line of approach. The only exceptions were talks given to small old-fashioned village groups where there was a high proportion of real country people. 'Happy Circles' and other similar social groups yielded much more information than either Women's Institute groups or town and city societies. Village groups, predictably, were richer sources of information than city groups.

The numbers of informants located from these five different sources are summarised in Table I, below:

TABLE I: SOURCES OF INFORMANTS

Source of Informants	*No. of Informants*
1. Local Radio (two programmes)	14
Local Television (1 appeal, 1 bulletin)	0
2. Local Press (4 articles)	23
3. Word-of-mouth, including village shop	38
4. Women's Institute (12 branches contacted plus 2 talks and 1 appeal in magazine)	5
5. Talks given to small local groups (not WI)	
4 'town-based'	0
2 'village-based'	9
Total number of informants	89

The way in which information is sought is of great relevance in locating suitable informants, as the following pages will seek to show.

The author has found that the so-called 'Hoover' approach is a very useful one. Rather than limiting conversation to plant remedies, it has proved far more fruitful to encourage people to chat about their childhood and life in the country. Many individuals who have categorically denied any knowledge of plant remedies, have then gone on to describe parts of their lives and in the course of this a great deal of information about remedies for illness in themselves and their animals has emerged. These remedies were obviously taken completely for granted as a necessary part of pre-Health Service life in the country.

The 'chatting' approach is obviously much more time-consuming than the use of questionnaires, but it has proved very productive, as well as enjoyable, and can be used in many circumstances where the use of a questionnaire would be totally inappropriate and off-putting. George Ewart Evans has described this finding in his own felicitous style:

> Old men who are full of memories may be like books, but you can't open them where you like. It was best – I found – to listen and let them talk, roughly in the area where I wanted their talk to be.[10]

Where individual informants were concerned, the author has not used questionnaires. However, one area of this study in which the questionnaire has proved very valuable is a small survey of schools in Norfolk. This is reported more fully elsewhere.[11] With help and co-operation from Gressenhall Rural Life Museum, a simple questionnaire was sent to a number of local primary schools. Children were asked to contact elderly friends or relatives and note down their childhood remedies for a variety of ailments. A lot of information was forthcoming, suggesting that this approach should be extended.

The questionnaire did not specify that only plant remedies should be recorded. As a result, much of the information returned concerned such domestic remedies as the wash-day blue bag for insect stings and bread poultices for boils. The reasons for asking simply for home remedies were twofold: all home remedies have their own intrinsic interest; in addition, the author has noticed that in chatting to people, if knowledge specifically of plant remedies is requested, this is seen as specialist knowledge, and many people will disclaim any such knowledge, even though they do know of many homely remedies, some of them using plants.

Forty-eight out of sixty-three returned questionnaires did include plant remedies and these provide a body of information interesting to compare with that from the eighty-nine informants found by other approaches.

Each questionnaire was completed by one child, whose source of information was usually one individual (grandparent etc) or a married couple. In this sense, a questionnaire is comparable with an individual informant (who would often include information from their spouse).

TABLE II: COMPARISON OF DATA RECEIVED FROM INDIVIDUAL INFORMANTS
AND SCHOOLS SURVEY QUESTIONNAIRES

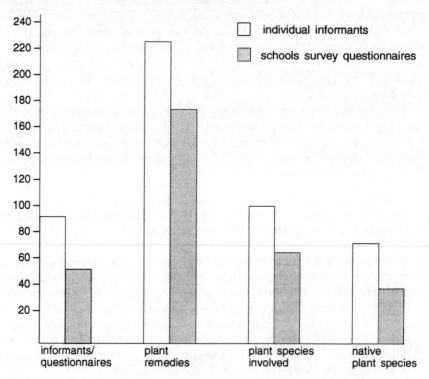

The Findings

Tables II and III summarise the findings from the group of eighty-nine individual informants, and the forty-eight questionnaires from the schools survey. The
figures show several interesting points. The data received by the two methods is
broadly similar in terms of information yield per person (Table III). Most
people remembered one or two plant remedies; relatively few had a large
number to report. This agrees with the findings of others, e.g. Jones in Wales.[12]

One significant difference emerges between the two bodies of data, and this is
the proportion of remembered plant remedies which involve native plant
species. Among the individual informants' remedies, 70% involved native plant
species, whereas, in the schools survey, the equivalent figure was 53%. This is a
statistically significant difference.

Authentic domestic remedies employ cheap, readily-available ingredients
and, where plants are used, they tend to be species that can be gathered in the
wild. This is in contrast to the official practice of herbalism, which in this
country uses a large number of foreign and, in particular, North American
species.[13] To some extent the proportion of native plant species in a collection of

TABLE III: YIELD OF INFORMATION PER INDIVIDUAL: COMPARISON
BETWEEN INDIVIDUAL INFORMANTS AND SCHOOLS SURVEY QUESTIONAIRES

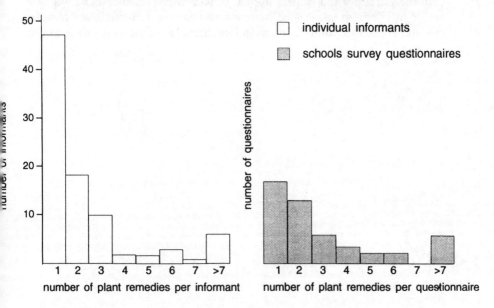

plant remedies reflects their authenticity as domestic plant medicine, and can
help to distinguish traditional plant medicine from what Dom Yoder has called
'the often observed phenomenon of a prosperous middle-class harking back to
herbal remedies'.[14]

In this present study, when choosing individual informants there was a
certain selectivity: those with a 'book' knowledge of the subject were not
included. On the other hand, with the questionnaire approach it is not possible
to distinguish between first-hand empirical knowledge of plant remedies and
those learned from books. These latter remedies include a large proportion of
cultivated plants – 'herbs' in the commonly accepted culinary sense. This
probably accounts for the difference in proportion of native plants in the two
categories of data.

To summarise, where, as in this study, a particular type of information is
being sought, both the 'chatting' and the questionnaire methods are fruitful.
The former is far more time-consuming, but one can be more selective in the
type of information received. Since many informants initially denied any
knowledge of plant remedies, but on further chatting a lot of information
emerged, it is likely that questionnaires would draw false blanks in many cases.
Clearly there is room for both approaches.

The author, in view of her admittedly very limited experience, would suggest
that both methods should be used. Since the questionnaires are less time-

consuming, they can be sent in greater numbers and thus serve to cast a wider net in the hunt for informants.

In the search for individual informants, local press, radio and chatting with people in village shops, yielded more information on domestic plant remedies than did appeals for information from local branches of the Women's Institute.

CHAPTER FOUR

Discussion of similarities and differences

Taylor's data and that of the present author

I T IS NOW possible, having presented the plant remedies gathered in the 1920s by Taylor and in the 1990s by the present author, to compare the two bodies of information. The first point to decide is whether there is likely to be any overlap between the informants involved in the two groups of data. Taylor did not record the ages of his informants, so this can only be guessed at. His two main sources of information were East Anglian practising doctors, and members of branches of the Women's Institute. In addition, he questioned primary school children, but unfortunately few of the resulting answers seem to appear among his notes. The age span of Taylor's informants must be in the range between thirty and ninety, if we exclude the school children. It is unlikely that any of them, or their contemporaries, were still alive in the 1980–1990 period. So in terms of overlap of individuals or their contemporaries, there is unlikely to be any. However, in terms of shared memories, there may indeed by considerable overlap. How long is a person's memory? is an open-ended question, rather like the proverbial 'how long is a piece of string?' For a person's memories are composed not just of events and information received during their lifetime but also of the recollections of others, including those of an older generation. This was probably even more true in the past, when people relied much more heavily on the spoken word for both information and entertainment. Probably it was more true in rural communities than in urban ones, because there was more conversation between people who knew each other well. When a person recalls a plant remedy, or any other piece of information, he may, consciously or otherwise, be drawing on the experience of others older than himself. Even in the case of a remedy actually used by the informant, details of how it is used may be of a very much older generation than the current user. In considering the age and origins of an orally transmitted remedy, it is therefore not sufficient to simply know the person's date of birth, though obviously this is of interest. Ideally, one needs to know in addition, whether the remedy was actually used by the informant themselves, or by a close friend or member of the family, or whether it is a 'hearsay' remedy, of which the person has themselves no direct evidence.

Questions such as these can only be answered in a relatively small number of instances, where personal contact is made with the individual concerned, and they are willing to share this type of information, and can remember the necessary details. In a survey such as that conducted by Dr Taylor, we have only internal evidence to go on when it comes to judging the 'authenticity' of the plant remedies concerned. In some cases, where an actual letter has survived, it is evident that a particular remedy was actually used by the informant. The remedy for jaundice, using berberis bark, is an example:

> This remedy was tried on us all as children, when we had jaundice through the house by an old woman, Mrs Heyhoe, the then Vicar's housekeeper. We rather liked it . . . (B.J.B. & H.L.B., Heacham)

In many cases, the detailed nature of the recipe suggests a remedy that was actually used, rather than a hearsay remedy. One striking difference between Dr Taylor's collection of plant remedies and those collected by the present author is the relatively high proportion of Taylor's remedies which do have precise 'culinary' style recipes. Take for instance this remedy contributed by Wilby WI for appendicitis:

> Inflammation of appendix should be treated with elder and peppermint, and a compress wrung out of the same liquor applied to the bowels. If the patient has been troubled with constipation inject into the bowels one pint of elder tea, and one of hot water; thirty minutes after inject two quarts of hot water, and when the bowels have been entirely cleansed, cease the injections, continue the compress, and give repeated doses of the herb until a bath of perspiration follows; keep patient one temperature for twelve hours.

These precise instructions obviously apply to a remedy that has been actually used. Likewise, the following recipe from Thorndon WI provides detailed instructions:

> To protect animals against flies and insects, take four ounces of walnut leaves, four ounces of lobelia leaves and one gallon of boiling water. When cold, strain and add four ounces tincture of aloes. Sponge down daily.

Similarly, this cold remedy from Blythburgh sounds tried and tested:

> Put a large bunch of sage into a jug, pour over it one pint of boiling water, and the juice of one lemon, sweeten with two large tablespoonfuls of honey, cover with cloth till cold, then strain and bottle. One tablespoon may be taken very often.

The immediacy of these remedies contrasts with statements such as:

> Celandine decoction a cure for cancer e.g. of the liver. (Dr B., Lowestoft)

As one would expect, the remedies obtained by Taylor from branches of the Women's Institute include much more by way of practical details, than does the

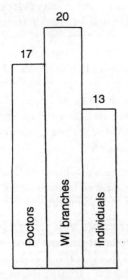

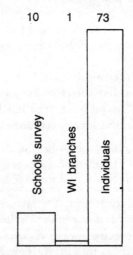

Taylor: Analysis of sources

Hatfield: Analysis of sources

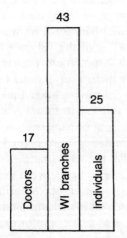

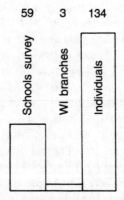

Taylor: Numbers of plant remedies
provided by these sources

Hatfield: Numbers of plant remedies
provided by these sources

information obtained from corresponding with doctors. This is not to suggest that the remedies submitted by doctors are invalid: but there is less evidence of their current usage. By definition, the remedies obtained by Taylor from his colleagues in the medical profession must fall into the category of 'hearsay' remedies. As we have seen in Chapter 1, medical services in rural parts of East Anglia in the 1920s were such that doctors would number very few of the poorest members of society among their patients, and it was precisely these people that would have had most need for cheap, easy home remedies as first aid. It could therefore be argued that many of the remedies submitted by doctors would have been not second-hand, but less direct than that. In one instance, the doctor recorded the source of his information:

St John's wort for bedsores, comfrey leaves, or houseleek, or marshmallow for inflammation as a local application. (The above were all communicated to me by a very shrewd old monthly nurse.) (Dr W.H.B., Lincoln)

When comparing Dr Taylor's collection of plant remedies with that made by the present author in the 1980s, it must be appreciated that neither collection is homogeneous. Taylor's collection embodies remedies from local branches of the Women's Institute, from East Anglian doctors, and from various private individuals. The present author's sources were branches of the Women's Institute, primary schools and private individuals. An analysis of sources, and yield of information per source, is shown in the accompanying diagrams, both for Taylor's collection of plant remedies and for that of the present author.

Although the numbers involved are too small to permit detailed statistical conclusions to be drawn several interesting points are at once apparent. As we have seen already, for Taylor's data, the richest source of information was the Women's Institute. It is not known how many branches of the WI were contacted by Taylor, but of those who responded with information, the average yield of plant remedies was approximately two per branch, a very similar figure to the yield per individual informant. The yield per doctor is lower (one per doctor). For the present author's data, the individual informants form by far the largest category, and again the yield of information is approximately two per informant. As mentioned at p. 66, the yield of information from branches of the Women's Institute was disappointingly small. From twelve branches contacted, only two informants resulted, numbering four remedies between them.

The results obtained from questionnaires sent to a number of primary schools cannot directly be compared with other sources of information, but are included here for completeness. The schools survey, as a source of information, has already been discussed (p. 67).

It is of interest that the yield of plant remedies per individual was much the same in 1920 and 1990. Then, as now, few people seem to have a wide knowledge of plant remedies: the majority have one 'favourite' remedy, or maybe two. There are a few individual exceptions to this rule, and these will be considered later.

It seems that sometimes a person learns one particular remedy at a time of personal or family crisis, and naturally remembers it for ever afterwards. Some examples of this will now be described. One lady, now in her eighties, vividly recalls the time when, it seems, her life was saved by a gypsy remedy. As a small child, she suffered from asthma, and during one particularly bad attack, she became so ill that the doctor was called (this was an unusual and drastic step, on account of the cost entailed). The doctor could offer her mother no comfort, and expressed the opinion that the little girl would not survive the night. Later that evening, a gypsy called at the door. She was known to the family, who had shown her kindness on an earlier occasion. Finding Dolly's mother in tears, she asked what the matter was, and on being told of Dolly's plight, gave the mother instructions on how to help. Here is the rest of the story in Dolly's words:

> I was only about four then, I suppose. I started school soon after that. She got to get all the little potatoes, and boil a saucepanful and then mash'em and get a piece of muslin and put'em in a poultice, then another piece of linen towel, not so that they'd burn, but so they're nice and hot, and put it on my chest back and front. An, well, the doctors give me up, they said I wouldn't live through the night – and then she did that, and then I tell yer I was making this awful noise to get my breath – you know, I couldn't get my breath, but when she put them on, after a few minutes that lifted – and d'you know I sat up and I was right relieved. Ooh, that was lovely to feel I could breathe again without making that awful noise, and that was all through these little potaters – and that's what she done and that relieved me, and I tell you the doctor came out at twelve o'clock and he couldn't believe his own eyes, because I sat up and talked to him and he couldn't believe it . . . and arter that I got on like a house on fire . . . but I never was so much trouble any more.[1]

Dolly did not have occasion to use this remedy again, but naturally she never forgot it. Another example of a plant remedy learned at a time of crisis also entails information from a gypsy. This incident took place in Middlesex, but the narrator subsequently moved to Norfolk. At the time in question, during the 1930s, her uncle was laid off work with very bad boils. There was no question of unemployment benefit, so money was particularly tight. When a gypsy called selling pegs and lace, her aunt explained the situation, and that she could not afford to buy anything. The gypsy suggested a bargain: if the aunt bought something, she would tell her how to cure her husbands boils. This was agreed and the gypsy explained how to make a groundsel poultice (p. 21). The results were dramatic, the husband returned to work, and the family not only remembered the remedy and recommended it to their new neighbours in Norfolk, they also found new uses for it, including the treatment of gout.[2]

There is no doubting the authenticity of remedies such as these, but information as complete as this is rarely available for any particular remedy. Remembered remedies are not always first-hand, some fall into the category of 'they used to use', or 'I've heard of people using'. Where the informant is contacted directly, it is usually possible to establish whether there is any direct evidence for the remedy actually being used. However, where the questionnaire approach is employed, as with the survey of primary schools, this distinction is rarely possible, especially since the information returned on any one questionnaire was often collected from more than one individual.

As discussed at p. 68, the questionnaire enables a wider net to be cast in the quest for information, but it does not necessarily yield information that is as accurate or reliable as that obtained directly from individuals.

In the author's own experience, chatting to elderly people was much the most productive and reliable way of obtaining information about plant remedies, but obviously it is also the most time-consuming. It was found that in many instances an acquaintanceship built up over a period of time led to more and more information being recalled. Two examples have already been mentioned (p. 65). An examination of Dr Taylor's notes suggest that one or two individuals wrote to him repeatedly, over a period of time, with new pieces of information (e.g. Miss G., Attleborough; Mrs S.B., who in one letter refers to herself as a 'Spitl Poor Visitor'). Then, as now, it seems that there were a few individuals with a wide knowledge of plant remedies.

The main differences between Taylor's data and that of the present author are:

1. More of Taylor's remedies take the form of actual recipes, with detailed instructions for use. This presumably reflects their *current* usage, as compared with many of the present author's collection which represent 'remembered' remedies.

2. A much higher proportion of Taylor's remedies were obtained from branches of the Women's Institute. The reasons for this have already been discussed at p. 66. Briefly, this difference reflects a change in population structure in East Anglian villages, which have now largely been taken over by 'incomers'. The East Anglian born-and-bred villagers are not only fewer in number than in Taylor's day, they tend to steer clear of local organisations which have been adopted by the newcomers.

Another obvious difference is the number of Taylor's remedies obtained from East Anglian doctors: this simply reflects the fact that Taylor wrote to a large number of country doctors in his quest for information. The present author has contacted only a relatively small number of doctors, and on the whole this has not proved a fruitful source of information. Patients nowadays do not tend to mention such things to their GPs. Indeed, one recently retired General Practitioner commented that, in his experience, if a patient had been using any kind of home remedy, the doctor would be the last person to hear about it! Many would fear the disapproval of their doctor if they admitted to the use of home remedies.

The fact that Taylor did obtain a lot of his information from fellow medical men suggests not that people were more ready in the 1920s to admit to the use of home remedies, but simply that such remedies were more widely used, and were to a greater extent 'common knowledge'. Although it cannot be proved, it is likely, as mentioned above (p. 62), that the remedies obtained by Taylor from doctors were not direct from the users of such remedies, but were relayed via wealthier patients to their doctors.

As to the type of plant remedy used in the 1920s and recorded in the 1990s, there seems to be very little difference in kind. Both collections of data include plants which were usually widely available, either growing in the wild or as cheap and readily available vegetables in an area that both then and now grows lots of vegetables. There were relatively few plants involved that were uncommon (thorn apple and marsh dock being two examples of relatively rare plants), and relatively few garden plants. Those garden species that were used in remedies were usually plants that one would expect to find growing in a cottage garden (e.g. culinary herbs such as sage, madonna lilies, berberis). Again, of course, there is the odd exception, such as the use of fresh fig leaves for warts, but in that case, when questioned, the informant explained that, as a child, she had a large fig tree growing in her garden, so the leaves were readily available.[3]

As regards the form in which these plant remedies were used, the only difference between Taylor's data and the present author's, is that poultices appear more often in the 1920s. Taylor records the use of the following plants in poultice form: houseleek (for bad breasts); carrot (for cancer); onion (for chest colds); narrow-leaved dock (for cancer); parsley (for boils); cabbage (for boils); chickweed (for 'general' poultices); turnip (also for 'general' poultices); bramble (for cancer); and feverfew (for toothache).

The present author has recorded the use of the following plants in poultice form: houseleek (for abscesses); onion (for earache and boils); chickweed (for eczema and dermatitis); linseed (for housemaid's knee and for quinsy in horses); sea lettuce (for arthritis); mallow (for boils); goosegrass (for ulcers); hot nettles and linseed (for lumbago); puff-ball (for carbuncles); groundsel (for boils and for quinsy in horses); hedge woundwort (for boils and carbuncles); potato (for asthma); comfrey (for broken wrists) and horse-radish (for lumbago).

Although the total number of plant species recorded in poultice form by the present author is higher (14 compared with 10), expressed as a proportion of the total plant remedies recorded, the proportion used as poultices is lower in the later collection. Approximately 12% of the plant remedies recorded by Taylor were used in poultice form, whereas only 4% of the remedies recorded by the present author were used in this form. This is in no way surprising: the use of a poultice is regarded by most people as a very old-fashioned treatment. There are still many people alive today who remember the use of bread poultices for everything from 'drawing' boils to easing sprains, but there are few people today who use them in self-treatment.

The commonest method of usage of plant remedies was the infusion. Approximately 42% of Taylor's plant remedies were used in this way. Approximately 35% of the present author's collection of plant remedies were used in this way. The term infusion in strict herbalist terminology means an aqueous preparation 'made by pouring boiling water over finely chopped botanical drugs',[4] whilst a decoction is made by 'pouring cold water onto the finely divided botanical drug and then allowing the mixture to simmer'. This method is used for hard materials such as roots and barks.[5] The distinction does seem to have been recognised in domestic medicine, but for the purpose of simplicity the two methods are grouped together here.

As the bar charts show, the overall picture for method of usage of plant remedies in the 1920s and the 1990s is remarkably similar. The figures have been expressed as percentages of total plant remedies recorded, since the sample size is larger in the 1990s collection.

Infusions, decoctions and local applications together account for 66% of Taylor's plant remedies, and for 63% of the present author's collection. This probably reflects the simplicity of these methods of preparation, compared, for instance, with the time-consuming process of making an ointment. It also reflects the first-aid nature of many of these remedies, where complicated methods of preparation would be inappropriate.

Now let us consider the range of conditions covered by Taylor's remedies and by those of the present author. As medical treatment has advanced during the century, and particularly as National Health Service medicine has become available to all, one might expect to find Taylor's collection of plant remedies used in the treatment of a wider spectrum of disease. For the purpose of this comparison, the animal remedies collected both by Taylor and the present author have been excluded, since there is still no National Health Service for animals!

The result of this comparison is at first sight surprising. There are relatively few ailments for which Taylor reports remedies which do not also appear in the present collection. Those ailments unique to Taylor's collection are: appendicitis, bedsores, consumption, sleeplessness and worms. On the other hand, the list of ailments covered in the present collection is much longer (61 ailments as compared with 31 in Taylor's collection). Any attempt at comparing the two bodies of information is made difficult by the different sizes of the two bodies of data. Thus Taylor described 86 different plant remedies, the present author 268 different plant remedies. Purely by chance, there is bound to be a wider range of ailments treated in the larger collection. Probably the only point of contrast worth making is that the present collection does not include remedies for consumption and appendicitis. The former is mercifully rare now, the latter would certainly not be treated nowadays by home remedies. The other differences are probably attributable to chance.

Although the diagnosed incidence of cancer is higher now than early in the twentieth century, the orthodox treatment for it has improved. Few people in recent times would experiment with home remedies for the treatment of a disease which is regarded with such fear. From this point of view, one might expect to find fewer cancer remedies among the more modern collection of remedies, but this has not proved the case. The numbers are, however, too small to draw reliable conclusions (both collections include four cancer remedies).

What does emerge from this attempt to compare Taylor's data with that of the present author, is the overall similarity of the two. Various, relatively minor, differences have been singled out. But overall, the two present a surprisingly similar picture of domestic medicine in East Anglia.

So what is the explanation of this overall similarity? The explanation seems to be two-fold. In the first place there is an overlap between remedies remembered in the last two decades, and those in use in the 1920s. Several recent informants recalled remedies used by their grandparents. The commonest age group of recent informants was 65–80, which puts the average date of birth of their grandparents at about 1880! Even where remembered remedies belonged to parents, rather than grandparents, the date of use of the remedy could still be around 1900. Even without knowing the ages of Taylor's informants, it becomes obvious that both Taylor, during the 1920s and the present author during the last few years, were tapping into the same reservoir of knowledge concerning plant remedies. This seems the most important explanation of the basic similarity between the two bodies of data.

The second explanation that could be postulated is the innate conservatism of domestic medicine. Where a traditional remedy has been used for centuries, it is unlikely to be changed quickly. This, of course, is a difficult point to prove.

To clarify these ideas further one would need a much larger body of more complete evidence. In an ideal world, one would need much more detailed information concerning each remedy: where, how, and by whom it was first used: whether the informant had first-hand experience of the remedy, or whether it was a 'remembered' remedy. In the real world, much of this information is not forthcoming, and it is certainly available retrospectively for Taylor's data. Where the present author has made personal contact with informants, it has sometimes, though not always, proved possible to answer some of these questions concerning a particular remedy. In the case of the following informant, his memory was excellent, and he was able to describe clearly his own experiences of plant and animal remedies, but even he could not tell where and when these remedies originated.

He was describing the use of ivy leaves as an animal tonic:

> Any good ivy, with a good bit of leaf, they'd eat it: if a cow didn't eat it, you'd know she really wasn't up to much at all and get the vet, but mostly if a cow was off colour and you'd give it a little ivy and a pail of water, away they'd go . . . Most of the farms round about here had a white hawthorn hedge, they're nearly all gone now, they were set there for a special purpose because the old men believed that if you threw the afterbirth up on to the hedge to dry, so the cow would heal up inside, or the mare would heal up and be that much better for it . . . If you had a calf that had diarrhoea . . . you used to give a whole egg, shell an' all, that would put'n right, also grind up a few acorns, that's what we did with the animals . . . If a cow knocked a horn off, the old cobwebs off the beams in the barn, dirty old thick old cobwebs, they'd wrap them round and that would stop the bleeding . . .

Whooping cough, one of the best remedies was to get a mangle from the farm, wash it well, leave the skin on, then slice it into big rings and lay it on a big meat plate and sprinkle over this a good lot of brown sugar and that'll make a syrup, the syrup used to drain to the side, two spoonfuls a day before you went to bed, that was a good thing . . . One of the best remedies I know of for a cold and still a good one is roasted shallots – we used to – with a stove, you know, the old-fashioned fireplace where you had a false grate in, you put those shallots in there whole, and let them roast underneath there, get them one at a time, cut the root part off, squeeze it out and eat that as hot as you can eat it – that would cure a cold and I still have them myself, roasted shallots . . .

Now I got a touch of rheumatism at the moment as you can see – that's age isn't it. I do know that we were cutting the hedge once and we were burning the old top, the green stuff off and one old lady come along 'You'll suffer for that, you'll suffer for that, you'll die wi' aching bones burning anything green. P'raps that's what I'm suffrin from.[6]

This informant was unusually exact in his memories. Many had much more fragmentary information, and time and again, it was heard that their mother/grandmother/aunt used all kinds of plants for all kinds of ailments, but the details were not recalled. We all of us take childhood experiences very much for granted. Presumably in the past, such knowledge was kept fresh because it was in constant use. In the majority of instances, although the plant remedies recorded by the present author had been used during the life-time of the informant, there was rarely evidence of their current usage. There were exceptions to this rule, and these will be discussed more fully in the following chapter.

But, on the whole, the remedies recorded in the 1980s were remembered, rather than currently used remedies. It seems likely that the present generation of elderly country people in East Anglia is therefore the last to possess any extensive knowledge of domestic plant medicine. It is therefore a matter of urgency to record such information whilst it is still available. Very little indeed of the information presented here has been written down by the informants, and apparently very little has even been passed down orally to the next generation. It is, quite literally, dying information, and once lost, cannot be recalled. It seems very likely that the same situation is true for other areas of Britain, and there is therefore an urgent need to record as soon as possible any remnants of knowledge of domestic plant medicine in Britain.

Little so far has been said about the 'local' nature of these plant remedies. For several reasons, this is an aspect of the study that is difficult to assess. Obviously, all the remedies presented here have been collected in East Anglia. But to what extent does this make them 'East Anglian' remedies.

There are insufficient comparable studies throughout the rest of Britain to make meaningful comparisons with other regions possible. Jones' records for Wales show many of the same plants in use there within living memory, and many are used for the same conditions (e.g. tansy for worms, ivy for corns, houseleek for eye conditions and for earache, coltsfoot for chest conditions, holly for chilblains, elderberry for coughs, blackcurrant tea for colds, and potatoes for sore throat).[7] Newman and Wilson in the 1950s reported some very interesting studies of plant remedies used in Lakeland and in Essex.[8] Among the Essex plants mentioned by these authors are cabbage, horse-radish, celery, mallow, tansy, chickweed, nettle, dandelion, goosegrass, wormwood, agrimony, scabious, lavender, and saffron, all of which appear too in the current study.

It is premature to attempt an assessment, in botanical terms, of the 'local' nature of these plant remedies. Until comparable studies are available for the whole of Britain, such an assessment would have very little meaning. As already noted, most of the plant remedies involve very common wild plants and vegetables, which are also common throughout most of Britain.

A further point concerning the term 'local' remedies needs to be made. Even where such a remedy is known to be used locally, this does not necessarily imply a local origin for the remedy. The country population of East Anglia was relatively stable during the early years of this century, but it was not entirely static. In those few instances where it has proved possible to trace back the origins of a particular remedy, these have proved to have come from as far afield as Ireland (goosegrass for ulcers), Scotland (ivy leaves for burns), Middlesex (groundsel for boils). In the case of yarrow ointment, used for scratches and grazes, the remedy was used in Essex by the present informant's grandmother, herself of Irish extraction. The remedy then moved, with the family, to Norfolk. Probably no collection of plant remedies will ever be entirely 'local'. Again, detailed comparisons cannot be made until more regional studies have been done.

CHAPTER FIVE

Are rural plant remedies a thing of the past?

Discussion of the middle class resurgence of interest
in herbalism, and the distinction between 'official' herbalism
and traditional plant remedies

Are rural remedies a thing of the past? Much that has been said in the preceding chapters would tend to suggest that, at least for East Anglia, this is the situation. The vast majority of people in this area with knowledge of domestic plant remedies are in the 65–80 age range, and among these people, few now use these remedies themselves, even though they did in their youth. The reasons for this are obvious: official medical help is now freely available to everyone, so few will bother to make up home remedies for themselves. In addition, many of the wild plants that were once so common (cornflower, scabious, tansy), are now relatively scarce in our disappearing hedgerows. Even where they occur, many people would be reluctant to risk gathering them in the wild because of pollution from pesticides and traffic fumes. Even in relatively rural East Anglia, in many areas the traffic is too heavy to allow plant gathering along the verges. For all these reasons, a decline in the use of domestic plant remedies is inevitable.

It has already been pointed out (p. 80), that, in the experience of the present author, it is very rare for any of these domestic plant remedies to have been either written down or handed down to the next generation. Oral traditions generally are on the decline, as television and the media take over almost completely from the art of conversation. Even in East Anglia, not many people now have time for a 'mardle'.

It seems, sadly, that the use of domestic plant remedies in East Anglia, of the type described in these pages, might soon become extinct. However, another type of plant medicine, 'official' herbalism, is attracting an increasing number of followers. On the whole this is very much a 'middle-class' phenomenon, a kind of secondary 'back-to-nature' movement, which is only financially available to the better-off. It is ironical that, as traditional knowledge of our native plant medicine dies, it is being replaced by an imported brand of herbalism.

Many people are, quite understandably, concerned about the undesirable side effects of many of the drugs used in modern medicine, and this is undoubtedly one of the major reasons for the upsurge of interest in all forms of 'alternative' medicine, including herbalism, homeopathy and the so-called Bach remedies. All these are a world away from the type of domestic plant remedies once used so widely in East Anglia and form part of what Dom Yoder has called 'the often observed phenomenon of a prosperous middle-class harking back to herbal remedies'.[1]

Strangely, though, this secondary return to herbal medicine draws on a different reservoir of information from the one described in these pages. In order to appreciate this, it is necessary to briefly consider the sources of knowledge of plant medicine during the last few hundred years in Britain.

Up until the time of publication of the early herbals, all knowledge of plant medicine must have been preserved by word of mouth. Monastic manuscripts were only available to the monasteries that produced them. Many of these were copied by much earlier sources which often involved the use of plants not native to Britain. One enterprising monk in the twelfth century seems to have substituted familiar species for their European counterparts when illustrating his herbal.[2] It seems highly likely that for the vast majority of the population, an orally preserved tradition of using easily available native British plants was the only form of herbal medicine available to them.

Even after the publication of the Herbals, these would not have been available to the vast majority, who could not read. Doubtless these herbals did influence the practice of domestic as well as official medicine, as this delightful story from the Highlands of Scotland shows.

Adam Donald was born in 1703, in Bethelnie, twenty miles north of Aberdeen. Ten years after his death, an account of him was published by Dr William Anderson in *The Bee*, a journal founded by the doctor. This account, though cynical and unkind, has at least the virtue of being contemporary. From birth, Adam was sallow and mis-shapen, so that local legend suggested that he was a changeling, substituted by the fairies. He grew up to be an awkward, gangling man, with little ability for the hard physical labour of his friends and neighbours. Anderson tells us that:

> Though he could scarcely read the English language, yet he carefully picked up books in all languages that fell in his way . . . He delighted chiefly in large books that contained plates of any sort; and Gerard's large Herbal, with wooden cuts, might be said to be his constant *vade mecum*.

Adam built up a reputation as a physician. He was chiefly consulted in cases of lingering disorders . . . In these cases, he invariably prescribed the application of certain simple unguents of his own manufacture . . . His fame spread to the distance of thirty miles around him, in every direction, so that for a great many years of his life there was never a Sunday his house was not crowded with visitors of various sorts, who came to consult him either as necromancer, or physician. His fees were very moderate, never exceeding sixpence when no medicines were given.[3]

It is rare to have direct evidence of this sort of the interplay between folk medicine and the medicine of the herbals. Undoubtedly, both influenced each other. Gerard has numerous references to anecdotes of particular cures brought about by certain plants. With the advent of the eighteenth century, however, the relationship between domestic medicine and orthodox medicine began to change. As official medicine became 'rationalised', the official pharmacopoeias diverged further and further from the domestic plant medicine as practised by ordinary people. Simple plant medicines were still being used to treat a wide variety of ailments, while official medicine began to prescribe more and more costly polypharmaceutical preparations.[4]

It is interesting to note that a condition, on the part of the publisher, for the production in 1926 of Mrs Grieve's famous *Modern Herbal* was that North American plants should be included. Mrs Grieve had produced, from her home in Buckinghamshire where she was the principal of a Medicinal and Commercial Herb School, a careful series of monographs on individual herbs. When Mrs Leyel received some of these through the post, she realised that they would make an excellent book and it is thanks to the combined hard work and dedication of these two ladies that Mrs Grieve's comprehensive *Modern Herbal*, edited by Mrs Leyel, appeared in 1926.[5]

Mrs Leyel's knowledge of herbalism was drawn from her own famous library of books on the subject. It is no surprise to find, therefore, that the herbal which she edited includes mainly 'book' knowledge of herbalism, although Mrs Grieve does include some 'country' uses of native British plants. It is interesting to reflect that the history of herbalism in this country might have taken a slightly different course had Cape's not insisted on the inclusion of North American plants in the *Modern Herbal*.

Mrs Leyel did a great deal to keep herbalism alive during the inter-war period. In 1927, she opened the first Culpeper shop, selling herbal medicines, cosmetics and food. This was a great commercial success and led to the present chain of Culpeper shops. In 1936, she founded the Society of Herbalists, for practising herbalism through these shops. In 1941 the Pharmacy and Medicines Bill was passed, prohibiting the sale of most herbal medicines. The existence both of the Society of Herbalists, and of the National Association of Medical Herbalists (founded in 1864) was threatened by this Act. However, Mrs Leyel had influential friends, through whose support the Bill was modified to allow members of her Society to be treated by herbalists. The present Herb Society, now an educational charity, is the successor of the Society of Herbalists. The National Association of Medical Herbalists struggled on through the early 1940s to become, in 1945, the National Institute of Medical Herbalists, now a thriving school of herbalism.

The herbal knowledge and practice thus rescued by Mrs Leyel and others were very different from the country remedies described in this book. Official herbalism had to be paid for, and was therefore out of the reach of many. The clientele of herbalists was, and still is, largely middle-class. Many of the plants used in official herbalism are imported.

In contrast, the traditional plant remedies described in this book were used as self-medication, and nearly always used plants which could be gathered, free, in the wild, or which (like the vegetables used in cold medicines, etc.) were very easily available.

The tradition of domestic herbalism was forced underground, while official herbalism was persecuted by the medical profession (Green Pharmacy).[6] Ironically, when herbalism found favour again in Britain during the late nineteenth and early twentieth centuries, it was largely an imported North American brand of herbalism that became established. Present-day herbalists in this country use a large number of North American plants.

Meanwhile, the 'grass-root' plant medicine used as first-aid in country areas survived, out of necessity, and was preserved very largely by oral tradition. Some of this domestic medicine became incorporated into published books on domestic medicine, an increasing number of which appeared during the late nineteenth and early twentieth centuries. Doubtless this was not an entirely one-way system, and some remedies were 'imported' back into domestic medicine from printed books, and from other countries.

It seems that this process has now moved one stage further in East Anglia. Since the advent of the Health Service, the need for domestic medicine has largely disappeared, and one might assume that, in time, all knowledge of such domestic medicine would disappear. Indeed, it came as a surprise to the present author to find just how much knowledge of plant medicines still exists in this region. As has been pointed out, this body of knowledge rests largely with the over sixty-fives; so will it become extinct with the passing of their generation? Is the knowledge now remaining purely 'vestigial', and without future function?

There are, rather surprisingly, fragments of evidence to suggest that this is not the case, and that there may still be a future for a modified form of domestic plant medicine in East Anglia.

The traditional nature of domestic plant medicine has already been stressed, and certainly there is more continuity than change in the remedies used. However, it seems that in this field, as in any other surviving area of knowledge, there have always been some innovative individuals, ready to experiment with new remedies, or new versions of old ones. Presumably, this must always have been the case, otherwise new plant remedies would never have been added to the reservoir of knowledge.

This lovely description of one such innovative user of plant remedies comes from an informant in Wickford, Essex (date of birth 1925):

> Great-aunt Alice was a real, old Essex lady: tall and stately yet down-to-earth and always ready for a chat . . . It must have been during the late nineteenth century years in Rayleigh that Alice developed her knowledge of remedies and local 'cure-alls' that I remember her for. This would have been when most of the town's roads were unmade and patchy scrub-land would have covered huge tracts of what are now housing estates. Here

among the wild flowers and grasses she would have gathered various herbs in order to try a new cure, or relief, of some kind . . .

What used to impress me was her belief that for most ills there was a nearby remedy, e.g. nettle and dock, marsh-fever and willow aspirin.

Great-aunt Alice learnt many of her divers remedies from older relatives and friends but some were created by her own invention.[7]

From very early times, it seems to have been a widely-held belief that where there is a disease, there must also be a cure. Perhaps this reflects a classic optimism in the human race? Such a conviction has sometimes been bound up with religious belief, as expressed by the eighteenth-century botanist Dillenius:

It is certain that on account of the special providence of the creator, each region produces the particular plants needed to cure the sickness of the local population. It is due to Providence that the territory of Giessen contains a great number of lily-of-the-valley, wild thyme and artemisia, because the local inhabitants suffer from frequent headaches, hysterical complaints and catarrh, for the treatment of which these plants are convenient.[8]

A more cynical interpretation would be that when country people are ill they have, in the past, been forced to rely on medicines composed of plants that are readily available. The belief that plants can provide treatments for most common ailments must therefore have been a comforting one. It is perhaps a distortion of this long-held faith in the healing properties of plants which has given rise to the modern popular misconception that because plant medicines are 'natural' they are harmless. Country people were wiser than this in the past:

We were lucky enough to live in the country and have a grandmother who understood the healing properties of plants. 'All plants are useful,' she would say 'only their mis-use is evil.'[9]

If we accept that domestic plant medicine progressed through the centuries by a cumulative process, drawing on common knowledge, remedies told by others, and remedies imported or re-imported from printed sources, then one might expect to find a large number of plant remedies in common between different ages and different geographical areas. This does indeed seem to be the case. As far as twentieth century domestic medicine is concerned, information is too scarce to make a comprehensive survey. However, it does seem that the body of knowledge concerning plant remedies is not entirely static, as one might have supposed. In East Anglia at least, there are still a few individuals, who, like great aunt Alice are prepared to try something new.

In a subject which depends for survival on oral tradition, it is inevitably difficult to provide evidence of such an assertion. The few fragments of information that are available are all the more remarkable because they have come to light in this one small study, and must surely imply further undiscovered examples.

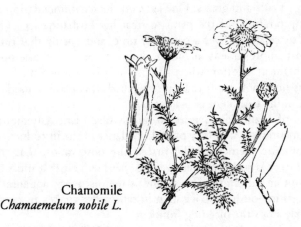

Chamomile
Chamaemelum nobile L.

One such innovative plant remedy involves the use of sugar beet leaves. The sugar beet (*Beta vulgaris, subsp cicla*), has been grown commercially as a crop for only about two hundred years in Europe.[10] In Britain, Essex was the first country to grow this crop in 1832 – a small venture which failed. In 1912 a factory was built at Cantley in Norfolk and although slow to develop at first, by 1953, nearly 100,000 acres were grown in the area. Compared with other vegetable crops grown in East Anglia, the sugar beet is a relative newcomer. It is therefore of particular interest to find that in Suffolk, the leaves have found a use in the treatment of erysipelas in pigs. Apparently when the leaves are fed to pigs suffering from erysipelas, the blisters disappear and the pigs improve rapidly.[11] In this instance, the remedy has already been told by one farmer to another, though how widespread it is is impossible to determine. How the original discovery was made is also not known.

Two other innovative plant remedies are of great interest in that both involve a chance discovery of a new use for a plant already used in both domestic plant medicine and official herbalism. The first concerns the use of chamomile, a well-known medical plant (*Chamaemelum nobile*). A lady working in a small herb farm in Suffolk suffered from psoriasis. She noticed that when her work involved hoeing between the rows of chamomile plants, her psoriasis improved dramatically. In the factory, she was involved with producing chamomile oil and during this process she had to collect the scum off the tops of great vats of simmering Chamomile flowers. She kept the scum that was removed and found that it greatly helped her psoriasis, used as an application. She eventually told her boss about this, and he gave her a bottle of the pure oil. She finds that, as long as she has a supply of the oil, she can keep the psoriasis at bay.[12]

The other chance discovery involves the use of goosegrass (*Galium aparine*). This is used in East Anglian domestic medicine in a number of ways. It has been fed to stallions in the spring 'to increase their seed'.[13] It was a frequent component of a spring tonic (often combined with nettles), and it has been used to aid the healing of cuts and grazes. One lady, on the recommendation of a friend, was preparing poultices of the plant to treat her husband's leg. The treatment continued (successfully) over a period of time, and during that time the lady noticed a great improvement in the psoriasis on her hands. She now uses the juice of the plant as a lotion when her psoriasis is troublesome.[14] In fact, although this was not known to the lady concerned, this plant is used in present-day herbalism in the treatment of psoriasis.[15]

Two other instances of chance discoveries do not involve plant remedies as such, but are worth a mention in that they provide evidence of the introduction of new ideas into domestic medicine. The first is the observation that the perfume 4711 applied to cold sores apparently cures them quickly.[16] It must be the actual 4711 and not an imitation! The second is the discovery, apparently made by factory workers in South America, that instant coffee makes an excellent styptic – i.e. quickly stops the bleeding from cuts.

Returning now to more strictly herbal domestic medicine, there are a few more examples of new versions of old remedies which are in current use.

One lady, now in her thirties and living in Suffolk, every year makes up a batch of what she and her family call 'Green Stuff'. Here is the recipe:

> Take one gallon of ground elder leaf, one gallon of comfrey leaf and 1 lb of vegetable fat. Boil until the leaves have disintegrated. Mix in some glycerine and put in jars for use.

This she and her family use as a first-aid treatment for cuts and grazes. The recipe is her own invention, based on the knowledge that comfrey is good for healing and ground elder is 'antiseptic'.[17]

She uses a number of other plant remedies as well, e.g. for treatment of worms in small children, an onion inserted into an itchy bottom apparently works wonders!

Another example of on-going herbal medicine comes from Kenninghall in Norfolk. A lady living there, now in her early fifties has brought up a large family and, wherever possible, has treated their ailments with plant remedies. It is particularly interesting to hear the sources of her information. The lady is not Norfolk born, but has lived in Norfolk for twenty-eight years. In that time she had collected information from elderly people in the area, from friends, relatives and from books. The remedies of which she has first-hand experience include the following:

> Elderberry syrup or blackcurrant syrup for colds; mint tea for colic; an infusion of coltsfoot leaves for coughs, or of horehound or mullein; ointment of comfrey root for cuts; sage tea or lemon balm tea for depression; an infusion of ribwort plantain leaves for diarrhoea; infusion of poppies for earache; raspberry tea for easing childbirth; yarrow tea for fevers and flu; valerian or chamomile infusion for sleeplessness; feverfew leaves eaten in sandwich for headache; garlic, sage and salt as an infusion to make a gargle

for a sore throat, milkwort infusion to increase milk supply when nursing; marigold ointment, or juice from the leaves for treating spots, including impetigo; a brew of plum, sloe and cherry bark for whooping cough; a raw clove of garlic every 2 hours while pain and fever last for sinusitis; for threadworm, garlic by mouth and in the anus, followed by a dose of epsom salts and juice of greater celandine for treatment of warts. For treatment of head lice in children, she had used a decoction of quassia chips.[18]

Some of these remedies are evidently learnt from books on plant medicine. Quassia chips, for example, appear in the British Pharmaceutical Codex[19] used as a bitter, and for the treatment of threadworms and as an insect repellent. This remedy is still used in official British Herbalism.[20] For many of these remedies, it would be very difficult to establish whether they represent 'primary' domestic medicine, or remedies re-imported into domestic medicine.

At a guess, and comparing these remedies with those obtained both by Taylor and in the present study, the following are probably representative of 'East Anglian Plant Medicine':

> elderberry syrup, blackcurrant syrup, coltsfoot and horehound infusion, plantain leaves, poppy infusion.

The remaining plant remedies could represent knowledge obtained from books or from official herbalism. This example highlights the impossibility of distinguishing between traditional domestic medicine and officially practised herbalism. In the opinion of the present author, such a distinction is likely to become increasingly blurred as the twentieth century draws to a close, and the generation of country-born East Anglians who had by force of circumstances to rely on plant medicine for first-aid, themselves die out.

The difficulty of distinguishing between domestic and official medicine is a subject that was discussed by Newman in 1947:

> Some so-called patent medicines or folk-cures contain regular medicinal drugs or active principles whose efficacy is well-known and tacitly accepted by medical men. The inclusion of old and well tried folk-cures in the pharmacopoeia was usually due to some physician having adopted it with good results, from the stock-in-trade of a village witch or wise woman. This instituted a double system of pharmacology, that is with similar drugs employed by both orthodox and unofficial practitioners . . .
>
> Thus the young mother who purchases a bottle of *Aq. Anethi Dest. B.P.* is not using a folk-cure, although she is doing so if an amateur pharmacist digests some cremocarps of Dill in a saucepan to make 'dill tea' for the baby's flatulence. The bilious person who purchased or was prescribed *Succ. Tarax. B.P.* (this, of course, before 1932, as the preparation was omitted from the sixth edition of the British Pharmacopoeia), was using an official cure, but if he dug up some dandelion roots and drank the expressed juice, he was employing a common folk-cure – 'a simple bitter – for a disordered liver'.[21]

Since this was written, the boundary between domestic and official medicine has become increasingly blurred. In addition, as noted above, there has been a largely middle-class, resurgence of interest in all forms of so-called 'alternative' medicine. The lady whose remedies have been collected over the past twenty-six years in Norfolk, has therefore drawn on an extremely old body of traditional knowledge concerning plant medicines, but has in addition incorporated knowledge from books on herbalism. Her own version of domestic medicine is therefore an inextricable mixture of folk medicine and book knowledge.

The story of the use of feverfew illustrates in a very vivid way the interaction between traditional and 'official' herbalism. As we have seen above, this plant appears in domestic East Anglian medicine as a remedy for coughs. In the old herbals, it was recommended by a variety of conditions, including fever and 'hemicrania', as migraine used to be called.[22] Recently, a publicised study of the use of feverfew in migraine was undertaken, funded by the Medical Research Council. The results were very interesting and encouraging, and as a consequence, freeze-dried preparations of feverfew are now widely available in this country.[23] [24]

In view of this, it comes as no surprise to find the use of feverfew for headache and migraine appearing several times among the home remedies cited in the schools survey described in Chapter 3. Here is a prime example of a traditional plant remedy used in this country for several centuries, whose use, at least in East Anglia, had become 'vestigial' (only recorded use in present study as a cough medicine; Taylor recorded its use as a poultice for toothache, see p. 54). Now, as a result of recent scientific study, its age-old use has been vindicated, and it is being re-introduced into both official and unofficial medicine. It seems that a large number of people, both young and old, are aware of the use of feverfew for migraine, and also for some forms of arthritis. A few years ago, one exhibitor at the Boat Show in London was selling small pots of feverfew. He was so impressed by the help he had gained from the plant, that he reckoned he was doing the world a good turn selling pots of it alongside his boats!

In the course of this chapter, several examples of innovative plant medicine in East Anglia have been cited. It is of great interest that recently an apparently new use for feverfew has been recorded in Norfolk. Presumably this is a chance discovery, resulting from the resurgence in use of the plant. It has now been found to be effective in the treatment of hot flushes during menopause, a use that is now being passed around by word of mouth.[25]

One last example of innovative current plant medicine in East Anglia will be given here. It concerns the use of mistletoe (*Viscum album*), a plant used at least since the time of the Saxons, who regarded the plant as sacred and deemed it a 'panacea against every disease'.[26] Pechey in 1694 recommended it for 'falling sicknes' (i.e. epilepsy, as well as giddiness and apoplexies).[27] Present-day herbalism recommends its use as a hypotensive (i.e. to lower blood pressure) and as an 'excellent relaxing nervine'.[28] One lady, now living in Colchester, regularly uses mistletoe, grown on apple trees in her garden. There is a family history of

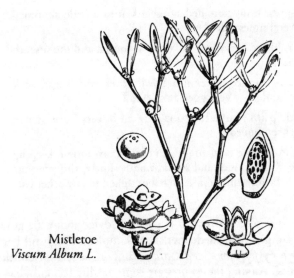

Mistletoe
Viscum Album L.

strokes, and both she and her father-in-law infuse a sprig of mistletoe in milk, overnight, and gently warm and drink the liquid the following day. This, it is hoped, will prevent strokes. The plant is dried for use during the winter. This is the only example which the present author has found of prophylactic plant medicine. The lady in question also uses various other plant remedies, e.g. chewing yarrow leaves for heavy periods.[29]

From what has been said in this chapter, it should by now be clear that, as has happened in the past, there is a continual system of feedback of information between traditional plant remedies, traditional herbalism, and present-day herbalism. It is impossible to separate out completely the strand of orally transmitted domestic plant medicine from the existing body of knowledge in official herbalism and in printed books. During the current century, and especially in the period between the wars, a large number of popular books on household remedies and recipes appeared. These are the subject of a current on-going study. It is already clear that such books did record many plant remedies in current use (e.g. the use of onions for treating colds). They also drew on earlier printed sources, and on folk medicine from other countries, as well as newspaper articles and magazines, catalogues of herbal companies, etc. Actual sources are rarely quoted, so that the only way of ascertaining the origins of such material is by a comparative study. This is not as yet complete.

Here are a few examples of remedies which appeared in books of household remedies between the wars, and which are readily identified with similar plant remedies used traditionally in the country. It should be pointed out that these have been selected: the majority of the remedies involve bought ingredients, including in many instances laudanum. Such remedies are presumably modifications of 'official' or of patent medicines.

Erysipelas. Put the juice from pounded houseleek into a little skimmed milk. Bathe parts several times a day.[30]

The rough side of a cabbage or ivy leaf will draw a wound, and the smooth side will heal a wound.[31]

Cut up a few slices of turnip, place in a bowl, cover with sugar, soak overnight. Bottle the liquid . . . Very good for a cold.[32]

To alleviate rheumatic pains. Bathe the parts affected in very hot water in which potatoes have been boiled.[33]

Wasp stings in the throat. The best thing is to chew a raw onion, keeping the pulp at the back of the mouth and swallowing it slowly; this prevents the throat swelling. N.B. Raw onion juice may be applied to any other part when stung.[34]

Gardening books of this period also frequently contain advice about the growing and preparation of simple plant medicines. For example, a delightful book called *The Woman's Treasury for Home and Garden* contains a section entitled 'Cures for Small Ailments'. Among these cures are some readily recognisable as traditional country remedies, e.g.:

Houseleek for corns and warts. The fresh juice of the common houseleek, (*Sempervivum tectorum*), applied night and morning to corns or warts, will cause their disappearance. the best method of application is to break the succulent leaves singly from the rosette growth of a plant and touch the callosity with the severed edge, meanwhile forcing out the sap by finger and thumb pressure.

Plantain leaves for stings. When stung either by nettles or by bees, wasps or mosquitoes, take the fresh leaves of common plantain (*Plantago major*), and after bruising them slightly, gently rub the affected part. This will afford great relief from the pain . . .

Strawberry leaf tea. The leaves of strawberries wiped clean and scalded with boiling water – one ounce of leaves to a pint of water – make a drink which is effective in cases of diarrhoea in young children. One teaspoonful is sufficient dose at a time, and it may be repeated at intervals of two or three hours while necessity continues.[35]

Although not dated, this book, from internal photographic evidence, clearly belongs to the period between the two world wars. The fact that so many books on domestic matters written at this time include simple plant remedies is further evidence for the widespread use of such remedies. The further scrutiny of such books is part of an ongoing study.

There is nothing new in this evolutionary process of the development of domestic plant medicine. The authors of the early herbals drew on information from earlier written works as well as on their everyday experience of the action of plant medicines, and on the experiences of others. During subsequent centuries the process of copying, borrowing and modifying continued. With the

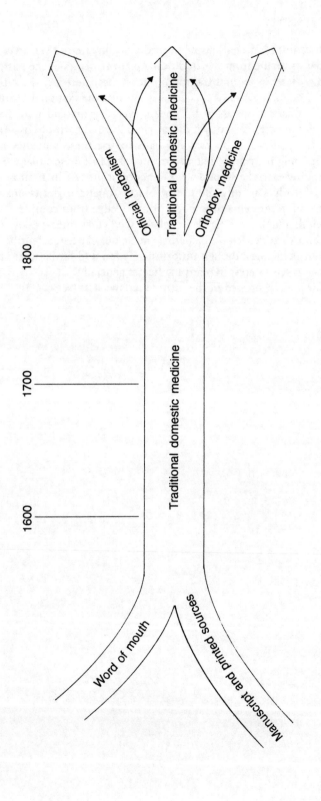

eighteenth century 'rationalisation' of medicine, an attempt was made to disso-
ciate official medicine from the traditional plant remedies of the past, but these
continued, at least as an oral tradition, out of sheer necessity in country areas,
right up to the early years of this century. Whilst the National Health Service
reduced the financial necessity for cheap, everyday first-aid remedies, knowledge of such remedies has not yet disappeared in rural parts of East Anglia.

As the last generation of East Anglians to use these remedies enter their
eighties, one might assume that the extinction of domestic plant medicine is
imminent. However, the secondary resurgence of interest in 'natural' medicine,
although it involves mainly the use of North American plants, may have the
effect of rescuing the remaining body of knowledge from complete extinction,
as those individuals interested in plant medicines incorporate traditional
remedies into their repertoire of herbal medicine. Current scientific studies of
British plant medicines, though unfortunately few and far between, might also
serve to re-awaken interest in plant medicines generally.

These ideas are expressed in the form of a flow chart (see p. 93).

CHAPTER SIX

A possible future for traditional plant remedies

The use of oral history in pinpointing potentially useful medicinal plants

IT SEEMS, THEN, that traditional plant medicine, as practised in East Anglia and in other rural parts of Britain, is on the verge not of complete extinction, but of being assimilated into present-day herbalism. This is foreseen by a lady, now in her seventies, now living in Essex:

> I was born in 1920 and spent my childhood in a mining village, the rows of terraced houses facing each other across cobbled streets. Every neighbour knew each other, shared their troubles – their happiness – their sickness. Illness was consulted, decided and often treated without calling in the local GP. The 'Head Consultant' lived at No. 73, a white-haired, long white bearded old man by the name of Christmas Davis. Yes, that was his real name. Children held him in awe and I can visualise him now sat in a wooden arm chair always smoking a clay pipe. He had a philosophy that there was a herb for every illness known to mankind. All mothers to be were prescribed an infusion of raspberry leaf tea, taken throughout their pregnancy for an easy delivery; parsley tea for bladder troubles, thyme for nerves, indigestion and stomach acidity, wormwood tea for a tonic and depression, sage tea for the menopause, chamomile tea for headaches. The strange thing was that very often the herb prescribed for falling hair was very often the same as for some other ailment. No matter of argument, the afflicted had faith in these remedies, believed in them and found relief in their usage. I think I saw the start of Alternative Medicine in those early days![1]

This type of plant remedy was the city equivalent of the plant remedies described in this study for East Anglia. In the city, plant remedies could only be prepared from dried herbs from the chemist, or from culinary herbs grown in small town gardens. In a fascinating anthropological account of folk medicine in Ireland, Nolan gives this telling quotation from an informant who was asked if we are witnessing a revival of folk medicine in Ireland. He replied: 'No, I would not say we are seeing the rise of Irish folk medicine; the fact is that it never went away'.[2]

Perhaps the same could be said for country parts of England and certainly for East Anglia. As we have seen in the preceding chapter (p. 91), those individuals in rural East Anglia who still use plant remedies, now draw on conventional herbalism as well as on traditional country remedies, so that the distinction between the two is likely to become increasingly blurred. Presumably as common hedgerow plants become less common, even country people will have to rely on bought herbs, or on those they can grow in their gardens. If traditional plant remedies disappear altogether, the total reservoir of knowledge concerning herbal medicine will be irreparably depleted. Knowledge of domestic plant medicine is part of our folk-lore heritage. It is also part of our medical knowledge, and for this reason too it is very important that it should be rescued from oblivion.

Orthodox medicine is often apt to overlook the debt it owes to folk medicine, and yet, as Oliver Wendell Holmes pointed out:

It (medicine) learned from a monk how to use antimony, from a Jesuit how to cure agues, from a friar how to cut for stone, from a soldier how to treat gout, from a sailor how to keep off scurvy, from a postmaster how to sound the Eustachian tube, from a dairymaid how to prevent smallpox and from an old market-woman how to catch the itch-insect.[3]

It is sad, then, to read comments like the following, coming from a member of the medical profession. Speaking of country cures and remedies, Dr Speller maintains:

There is little in these bizarre and entertaining 'cures' that can have any basis in therapeutics. The foxglove story is one of the few instances where a country remedy has proved to contain an active pharmacological substance. Most of them are to be regarded as superstitious and magical, with success by the patient's belief, or by chance, or not at all . . . Even today remedies have followers. Country doctors find shadows of ancient cures used alongside prescribed treatment and while their total rejection and redundancy were accelerated by the advances of nineteenth century medicine – the germ theory of disease, scientific nursing, X-rays, anaesthesia, asepsis – and later by the establishment of the National Health Service, it may be years yet before it is completed, although in general the heyday of the folk-cure had passed by 1914.[4]

What a lot of irreplaceable information we could lose if this attitude were generally adopted.

Surely the attitude of the doctor who wrote to Dr Taylor in the 1920s is a wiser one:

It's difficult to decide what a cure charm is – most of our own nostrums will come under this head in a few years![5]

The same idea is expressed very vividly by Mr B. from Boreham, at the end of a description of the home remedies he remembers from his youth:

Many must have been based on tradition, some on experience, and many on hope. In the light of present knowledge of the body and disease, many seem rather strange and the product of credulity. However, perhaps the poet Pope said it all when he wrote: 'We think our fathers fools so wise we grow. Our wiser sons will doubtless think us so.'[6]

In a paper delivered as long ago as 1947, Leslie Newman pointed out:

The clinical effects of many herbal folk-medicines are unknown and the active constituents (if any) have not been identified but it is possible that some useful additions to the list of official drugs will be made when our native flora is more fully investigated. A widely-used folk remedy for malaria or ague which, up to the last century, was common in the Eastern Counties as well as in other parts of Great Britain, was a pill made of spider web or of the spiders themselves. It might be imagined that this treatment was quite useless as a remedy and was merely a good example of the survival of folk beliefs with no reasonable basis . . . Yet in 1882 when Oliva isolated the principle arachnidin from spider webs, it proved an excellent febrifuge, and similar pills had saved many lives in Madras in 1867 . . . The actual therapeutic value of many of our herbal samples has long been a matter of dispute between pharmacologists and folklorists, and there seems little chance of any agreement between the extreme views of a large group of 'health' enthusiasts who follow blindly all modern cults, of folklorists interested in the types of country cures and the somewhat academic attitude of professional pharmacologists. The 'back to nature' exponents usually exhibit a touching faith in the opinions of herbalists and assume that all plants described in the older herbals possess the virtues attributed to them. The professional school, quite naturally, throw the burden of proof upon those who, from lack of training and adequate facilities, are unable to carry out the elaborate tests required to decide on the merits of any plant used in folk-medicine. It does not follow that because any 'herb' possesses a definite pharmacological value that it should be admitted to the Pharmacopoeia – there are often other and better remedies available. But it is obvious that some of the old country preparations of fresh or dried native plants – teas, poultices, wet dressings, infusions or decoctions – may possess a different action to pure alkaloids, tinctures and other official preparations.[7]

Since this was written, considerable progress has been made world-wide in the subject of ethnobotany, but the sad fact remains that our own native British flora has been largely neglected. It is precisely the kind of simple, inexpensive plant remedies described in this book which could prove of real therapeutic value in the future. Far from turning our backs on old-fashioned plant medicines, we should be investigating them as a matter or urgency, before knowledge of them is lost for posterity.

Periwinkle
Vinca major L.

A striking example of the kind of information hidden in folk medicine is to be found in the manuscript of the *Gunton Household Book* in Norwich. This was written in the late seventeenth and early eighteenth centuries by members of the Harbord family, of Gunton Hall near Lowestoft. On page 24 of this manuscript we read:

> For a sore brest yt is Painfull knotted and yet white and hard Take . . . ye herb Periwinkle, and fume it over frankincense and apply it hot morning and evening renew it as ye herb dryes away continue this for some time and it will take y pain away and disperse ye knots. Prov'd by Mrs Bacon of Ipswich.[8]

The periwinkle (*Vinca major*), naturalised as a garden escape throughout much of Britain, is a close relative of the South American species from which the so-called Vinca-alkaloids were first obtained. These drugs have revolutionised the treatment of leukaemia and are also used in the treatment of various other malignancies. Perhaps if Mrs Bacon's remedy had been more widely known, these therapeutic agents would have been discovered sooner.

Time and again there are examples of folk-medicine unofficially discovering remedies which only become official years later. The discovery of antibiotics is another well-known example. A lady now in her seventies, living in Essex points out:

> We had never heard of anti-biotics or penicillin but knew that wounds healed well if wrapped in cheesecloth with the mould still adhering.[9]

The story of an on-going study of a Norfolk plant remedy will now be described in some detail, as it will serve to illustrate many of the points made in the preceding pages. Because this work is at the present time the subject of a confidentiality agreement, the name of the plant concerned cannot at the moment be published. It will be referred to here simply as Plant X.

In the course of a radio phone-in programme in 1986, the present author was told of a plant remedy for the treatment of leg ulcers. Since this is a very common condition, and one moreover that is not readily cured by orthodox medical treatment, this was of particular interest.

The informant, Mrs P.B., is now in her fifties.[10] Her mother trained as a nurse in Bedford, and after her marriage moved to Sprowston. Here she soon developed a reputation as the person to turn to in times of illness, and she was frequently called upon for first-aid. From her mother, she had a wide knowledge of plant medicines, and she combined these with her training as a nurse. There was no doctor in the village at this time, but the nearest GP held a weekly surgery in one room of her house. He soon discovered that she had more success in treating leg ulcers than he did himself, and he began referring patients with leg ulcers to her. Mrs B. remembers as a child helping her mother to gather plants from the hedgerows that were used in the various medicines that she made.

For the treatment of leg ulcers, a poultice was made from freshly gathered Herb X. A handful of the spring-time shoots were washed, chopped roughly, and crushed lightly in a pestle and mortar. The crushed plant was enclosed in muslin to form a poultice, which was applied to the leg ulcer and changed daily. It was held in place with a piece of oiled silk.

Mrs B. remembers many elderly people with leg ulcers receiving this treatment, and all recovered. Her estimate is that she herself had seen about forty people cured in this way.

As Mrs B. grew up, she always remembered this particular remedy, and from time to time recommended it to friends. As a result of the radio programme, several sufferers from leg ulcers asked to know about this remedy, so that they could try it. This immediately posed several very difficult ethical problems. It is not permissible to recommend officially, as it were, a remedy that is not officially approved. Before such a remedy could be officially approved, there would have to be a significant body of evidence of its clinical success. This could only be obtained if people were willing to try the remedy, and, understandably, few people are willing to try a 'new' remedy for something as serious and painful as a large leg ulcer, without the approval of their GP. The GP, in turn, could not give his official blessing to an unproven remedy. It seemed a case of stalemate.

There were, however, a few brave individuals who were sufficiently desperate to try almost anything. They were all people who had received orthodox treatment for their leg ulcers, but without success. It was decided that these people, who were willing to shoulder the responsibility for their own treatment, would be told the details of the remedy. Since quite large amounts of the plant were needed, help was given in harvesting the plant from areas free from agricultural pollutants.

Traditionally, the plant should be gathered in the springtime, whilst the shoots are still growing, and before the plant seeds. Unfortunately, leg ulcers are not seasonal, so one immediate problem was to develop a method of preserving the plant which would not affect its healing properties. It was found that the plant could be kept in the salad compartment of a fridge for up to two weeks without losing its therapeutic properties.

A handful of people who tried the remedy at this stage found it to be highly effective. A bonus of the treatment seemed to be that the poultice was soothing and they were able to sleep better. One man,[11] had had a large leg ulcer for more than two years. It began to heal within six weeks of starting the treatment, and was completely healed within three months.

It soon became evident that here was a remedy worth investigating further. Before a clinical trial could be undertaken, it was necessary to do a thorough literature search, to find out the state of knowledge concerning the plant. It was also necessary to adapt the method to a hospital setting. Plant poultices are unacceptable in a modern hospital, even though, as one consultant pointed out, a microbiology survey in London showed the hospital wards to be more heavily infested than the hospital car park!

The literature search began. In an attempt to discover the possible origin of the remedy, numerous books on herbalism were consulted. Meanwhile, in the course of the primary schools survey of plant remedies in Norfolk, an interesting fact had come to light. Another informant reported the use of the same plant X on leg ulcers.[12] This person described exactly the same remedy, and added that it had been told to their family by an Irish friend. The pieces of the jigsaw now began to fit together. The author's attention was drawn to an Irish book published nearly eighty years ago:

> The Plant X was used as an application to ulcers, and was especially used for cancerous growths that had ulcerated surfaces. It was cut up and applied *en masse* to the affected surface. The juice was given internally at the same time.

The Irish connection was strengthened further by the discovery of the following article which appeared in a late nineteenth century medical paper:

> ' "Plant X", a Remedy for Chronic Ulcers', by F.J.B. Quinlan, MD. Dubl, Physician to St Vincent's Hospital . . .
>
> Few of those connected with the admission of patients into hospital fail to observe the number of applicants suffering from chronic ulcers, principally of the legs; and in some institutions there seems to be a tacit rule against their admission. When admitted, to especially if old and broken-down persons, they frequently occupy a bed for months, to the exclusion of relievable sufferers, and sometimes with unsatisfactory results. The great difficulty in treatment seems the impossibility of maintaining permanent healthy granular action; and strapping, sponge-grafting, skin-grafting and

the application of irritants, such as mercuric oxide, silver nitrate, or cupric sulphate, are often tried in vain. I would wish to mention a remedy new to me and which proved successful when all the above well-known methods had entirely failed.

Immediately after the publication in the Journal of January last of a note upon a pulmonary remedial sample, I received letters from several parts of the United Kingdom, recommending me to try the effects of the Herb X in the treatment of chronic ulcers – a recommendation which I was unable to adopt, for the sufficient reason that the plant was then nowhere to be obtained. I made a note of the matter and a suitable opportunity for trial presented itself in due time.

Cornelius C., aged 74, from Clonmel, a very tall, weak and worn-out old man, applied for admission to St Vincent's Hospital on the 8th of February last. He suffered from enormous ulcers of both legs; that on the right being eight inches and a half long and extending nearly round the whole limb; and that on the left being a little smaller. He had just come out of another Dublin hospital, where he had been for four months under the care of a very eminent medical man, and with no good result. A more unpromising case of such ulceration could not be imagined, and few hospitals would entertain the idea of receiving him. He was, however, admitted at the request of a very valued friend of the institution, who represented that he had come a long way from home in the hope of relief. Strapping being plainly out of the question, from the size of the ulcers and the low vitality of the surrounding skin, I grafted the entire surfaces with layers of sponge. This process went on in the usual manner, and left a healthy surface; the granulations of which, however, soon died away, and could not be kept up. Skin grafting failed utterly.

We had now come nearly to the end of April and our failure in this case was as complete as that of our sister hospital. It appeared to me that now was the time to try the Plant X, which was beginning to peep out in all the hedgerows about Dublin. Here I must tender my acknowledgements of the zeal and energy of the members of my clinical class, who were untiring in their efforts to collect this herb, which was not to be had of any of the herbalists. An ample supply for this and other less severe cases has since been kept up and it has been used with the most marked success in the following manner.

Grasping in the left hand a bundle of ten or twelve stalks, with scissors held in the right hand, the bundle is cut into chunks about half an inch long. These are thrown into a mortar and pounded into a paste. This paste, which has an acrid taste and slightly acrid smell, is made up into a large poultice, applied to the ulcer and secured with a bandage. It is renewed three times a day. Its action appears to be a slight steady stimulant and powerful promoter of healthy granulation. Its effect in this most unhopeful case was decisive and plain to all. Healthy action ensued and has since steadily continued; and, after a month of treatment, both ulcers have been reduced to considerably less than half their original size. If this action continues, which I have no reason to doubt, the cure will be accomplished in a measurable and short period. The patient is in the ward and anyone can see the great amount of new dermatisation which has been effected during the month.

[Here other cases are quoted.]

My reason for putting forward this remedy so soon is, that now is the time to try it. It is growing freely in almost every hedge and can be got in any quantity during the rest of the season.

A difficulty at once suggests itself as to its general employment; viz that in winter and spring it is not to be had at all. It appears to me that this difficulty can be effectually met by the method of ensilage, by means of which green food for cattle has for the last few years keen kept perfectly sweet and fresh by burying it in silos under the ground . . . One of my pupils, Mr M Piece, has already laid it thus down, and will report the result to me . . .

Many virtues are attributed to the Plant X by old writers; but I have not been able to find any allusion to its employment in the treatment of ulcers.

This paper has been quoted at length because it contains many interesting points. Clearly, in 1883, the use of Plant X poultices was a traditional remedy which did not appear in the literature of the day. Moreover, the method used is exactly the same as that reported in 1986 by Mrs B. to the present author. A hundred years later, it still seems to hold true that this remedy does not appear in the herbal literature. It seems that this is a prime example of a plant remedy used by country people and kept alive by oral tradition. The accuracy with which it has survived is a tribute to the reliability of oral evidence.

The plant is used in modern-day herbalism, but not for the treatment of leg ulcers.[13] It is of great interest to note, however, that it seems almost as difficult now to obtain the plant from a herbal supplier as it was when Dr Quinlan tried a century ago. The present author was able to obtain dried supplies of plants gathered in Germany, but only in limited amounts. This again bears out the fact that the use of the fresh plant in treating leg ulcers has been and remains primarily a domestic remedy.

It would be inappropriate to detail here the state of knowledge concerning the pharmacology of this plant. Like many of our common wayside plants, it has not been thoroughly analysed. However, the plant is known to contain iridoids, including asperuloside and asperulosidic acid. This is present in higher concentrations in the actively growing internodes of the plant. When the plant is crushed, the asperuloside breaks down to coumarin and glucose. The coumarin is one probable active principle in the plant's healing effect on ulcers.

The traditional way of using the plant, namely crushing the fresh springtime shoots and applying, is therefore vindicated by chemical studies to date. Here surely is evidence that it would repay us to look seriously at some of our native British plant remedies, before knowledge of them disappears for good.

Currently work is under way to modify the traditional method of use of this plant is such a way as to render it acceptable in a hospital setting. This has to be done without damaging the activity of the plant. This work is at the moment the subject of a confidentiality agreement and cannot as yet be reported in full.

Before leaving the subject of this particular plant remedy, one last anecdote will be related because it highlights the discrepancy between the old ways and the new. One enlightened GP heard about the present author's interest in leg ulcers. One of his patient's, an elderly man, had suffered for many years with leg ulcers on both of his legs. With the agreement of the patient, who himself was interested in plant remedies, it was proposed to treat one leg with the plant remedy, the other with continuing orthodox treatment. All went well and the plant-treated leg began to show marked signs of improvement. Then, one day, the nurse called to change the 'orthodox' dressing on his leg while the plant treatment was under way. She was a young, newly-qualified nurse; she took one look at the plant-treated leg. 'It's green!' she shouted, 'It's gangrene!' The author explained that the green colouration was due to the plant juice, but the nurse was deeply unhappy, and so by then was the wife of the patient. The nurse insisted that skin cultures should be taken from the leg to test for infection. This was of course agreed, and samples were sent off from both legs to the pathology laboratory. Those from the plant-treated leg came back as negative, whilst all sorts of bacteria were growing on the 'orthodox' treated leg. The nurse could not accept this result and repeated the tests, with the same outcome. Unfortunately by this stage, the wife of the patient had become thoroughly alarmed and the plant treatment to the disappointment of the patient, had to be discontinued.

What the present author did learn from this story, is that any present-day studies of traditional plant remedies have to be undertaken in a highly or-ganised and official manner. The gulf between official medical practice and home remedies has been widened by the increasing fear on the part of practi-tioners of being sued if the outcome is unfavourable. Under these circum-stances, it is readily understandable that no modern medical practitioner feels able to accept responsibility for an unorthodox treatment of his patients.

This study is now proceeding slowly along official lines and the research protocol has been submitted to the local District Ethics Committee. If ap-proved, it is hoped that a small pilot clinical study will begin at a local hospital in Spring 1993.

This study is in no way unique. Plant remedies throughout the world are now under scrutiny in the search for further medicinally useful plants. The reason that it has been reported here in some detail is that the present author is involved with the study and it is unusual in that the story of its adoption from traditional domestic medicine into (hopefully) current medical practice is there-fore fully known. Numerous plants that are used in official herbalism through-out the world are now being studied, and it seems that many will yield medically valuable drugs. The clinical trials of feverfew have already been mentioned.[14] Studies of Garlic and on onion,[15][16] seem set to vindicate some at least of the traditional uses for them. Dr Caroline Day, at Aston University, has undertaken a survey of traditional plant treatments for diabetes.

> Some compounds are showing promise . . . They appear to have different modes of action to those of current oral hypoglycaemics and they could have better safety profiles.[17]

On this hopeful note, let us leave the subject of East Anglian Plant remedies and trust that in the future our humble domestic medicines will receive the attention they deserve, so that they can be preserved as part of our national heritage, and as a reservoir of knowledge for future searches for medicinally valuable plants.

NOTES

CHAPTER ONE

1 C.B. Hawkins, *Norwich, A Social Study*, Philip Lee Warner, 1910, p. 270.
2 M.A. Crowther, *The Workhouse System, 1834–1929*, Methuen, 1983, p. 3.
3 Justin & Edith Brooke, *Suffolk Prospect*, Faber & Faber, 1963, p. 105.
4 *Report on the British Health Services*, Dec. 1937, PEP London, 1937, p. 255.
5 *Ibid.*, p. 262.
6 S. Cherry, 'Change and Continuity in the Cottage Hospitals c.1859–1948: The Experience in East Anglia', *Medical History*, 1992, 36, pp. 271–289.
7 C.B. Hawkins, *op. cit.*, p. 277.
8 M. Muncaster, Ph.D. Thesis, University of East Anglia, 1976, p. 74.
9 J. Young, *Farming in East Anglia*, David Rendel, London, 1967, p. 19.
10 E.L.A., Essex, d.o.b. 1915, Age Concern essay (unpublished).
11 Mrs T.C., Essex, d.o.b. 1918, Age Concern essay (unpublished).
12 S. Cherry, 'Beyond National Health Insurance, the Voluntary Hospitals and Hospital Contributory Schemes: A Regional Study', *Social History of Medicine*, Dec. 1992, pp. 455–482.
13 PEP Report, *op. cit.*, p. 211.
14 M. Penelope Hall, *The Social Services of Modern England*, Routledge and Kegan, 1952, p. 67.
15 Mrs M.S., Essex, d.o.b. 1914, Age Concern essay, 1990 (unpublished).
16 R. Blythe, *Akenfield*, Guild Publishing, 1980, p. 200.
17 *Suffolk Prospect, op. cit.*, p. 209.
18 PEP Report, *op. cit.*, p. 143.
19 Miss S., Forncett End, via Mrs B., Tacolneston, Norfolk, personal communication, 1988.
20 A. Armstrong, *The Farmworkers 1770–1980*, Batsford, 1988, p. 196.
21 D.C.H., Essex, d.o.b. 1926, Age Concern essay, 1990, p. 196 (unpublished).
22 A. Jobson, *Victorian Suffolk*, Hale, London, 1972, p. 82.
23 Mrs P.B., Sprowston, personal communication.
24 Mrs A.A., North Walsham, Norfolk, personal communication.
25 Mrs I.H., Flordon, Norfolk, d.o.b. 1920, personal communication.
26 Mrs D.T., Rockland St Mary, Norfolk, d.o.b. 1910, personal communication.
27 Mrs A.P., Great Plumstead, Norfolk, personal communication.
28 Mr D.H., Lowestoft, personal communication.
29 F.C. Wigby, Norwich, personal communication.
30 Elizabeth Harland, *No Halt at Sunset: The Diary of a Country Housewife*, Benn, 1951, p. 82.
31 Jack Overhill, 'White Magic', *East Anglian Magazine*, June 1975, no. 8, vol. 134, p. 378.
32 H.C. Brundall, personal communication, 1990.
33 *Within Living Memory*, Norfolk Federation of Women's Institutes, 1972, p. 50.

34 Mr G., Hemsby, Norfolk, personal communication, 1989.
35 Mr W.G., Witton, Norfolk, personal communication, 1988.
36 Mrs V.M., Brundall, Norfolk, personal communication, 1988.
37 Mrs E.F., Gt Waltham, Essex, Age Concern essay, 1990, unpublished.

CHAPTER TWO

1 See Obituary, *British Medical Journal*, 2, 1942, p. 175.
2 Dr Mark R. Taylor 'Folk Medicine in Norfolk', *Folklore*, 40, 1929, pp. 113–138.
3 Dr Mark R. Taylor, Norfolk Records Office, MS4322, 57 x 1.
4 F.C. Wigby, Norwich, personal communication, 1990.
5 *I Walked by Night*, ed. Lilias Rider Haggard, Boydell Press, 1974, p. 21.
6 Enid Porter, 'Some Old Fenland Remedies', *Education Today*, July 1964, pp. 9–11.
7 John Glyde, *The Norfolk Garland*, Jarrold, 1872, p. 34.
8 Walton Dew, *A Dyshe of Norfolk Dumplings*, London, 1898, reissued E.P. Publishing, 1973.
9 L.F. Newman and E.M. Wilson, 'Folklore Survivals . . .', *Folklore*, 62, 1951, pp. 252–266.
10 Mr G.G., Ludham, Norfolk, d.o.b. 1900, personal communication, 1988.
11 Dr Mark R. Taylor, *op. cit.*
12 Quoted in *Potter's New Cyclopaedia of Botanical Drugs and Preparations*, R.C. Wren, Health Science Press, 1975, p. 265.
13 John Buchan, Domestic Medicine, 3rd edn, 1774, p. 578.
14 *Ibid.*, p. 738.
15 Mrs M. Grieve, *A Modern Herbal*, Cape, 1931, p. 746.
16 Miss H.C. Colman, *Princes St Magazine*, Nov. 1924, p. 173.
17 Dr C.P. Petch, *Flora of Norfolk*, Jarrold, 1968.
18 George Ewart Evans, *The Farm and the Village*, Faber, 1969, pp. 112–113.
19 W.W., Bury St Edmunds, *East Anglian Magazine*, Dec. 1975, p. 125.
20 Privately-owned manuscript, Mr C.C., Norton Subcourse, Norfolk.
21 Unpublished essay for Age Concern, Essex.
22 'More Secret Remedies', British Medical Association, London, 1912.
23 Mrs A., Wicklewood, Norfolk, personal communication, 1989.
24 Notes of Dr Mark Taylor, *op. cit.*
25 Mrs H.S., Foulsham, Norfolk, personal communication, 1988.
26 *I Walked by Night*, ed. Lilias Rider Haggard, Boydell Press, 1974, p. 16.
27 Mrs B., Great Plumstead, Norfolk, d.o.b. 1910, personal communication, 1988.
28 Mrs V.W., Brundall, Norfolk, d.o.b. 1925, personal communication, 1988.
29 Mrs A.C., Aylmerton, Norfolk, d.o.b. 1900, personal communication, 1987.
30 Mrs F.S., Cley, Norfolk, d.o.b 1920, personal communication, 1988.
31 Mrs D.T., Rockland St Mary, d.o.b. 1910, personal communication, 1988.
32 J. Britten & R. Holland, *Dictionary of English Plant Names*, Trübner, 1878, p. 377.
33 Mr F.C.W., Wicklewood, Norfolk, d.o.b. 1910, personal communication, 1989.
34 Mrs V.C., Hoxne, Suffolk, d.o.b. 1925, personal communication, 1988.
35 Mrs M.S., Braintree, Essex, d.o.b. 1914, unpublished essay for Age Concern, 1991.
36 Mrs M. Grieve, *A Modern Herbal*, Jonathan Cape, 1931, p. 862.

37   *Potter's New Cyclopaedia of Botanical Drugs and Preparations*, R.C. Wren, re-written by Williamson and Evans, 1988, C.W. Daniel Co. Ltd, p. 289.

38   Mr H. Bedford, d.o.b. 1910, personal communication, 1987.

39   Mr D.B., High Easter, Essex, d.o.b. 1925, unpublished essay for Age Concern, 1990.

40   *Gunton Household Book*, MS in church of St Peter Mancroft, Norwich.

41   Mrs A.A., Walcott, Norfolk, personal communication, 1987.

42   Mr J.B., Essex, d.o.b. c.1915, unpublished essay for Age Concern, 1990.

43   Mrs E.J., Salhouse, Norfolk, d.o.b. 1907, personal communication, 1988.

44   Mr G., Ludham, Norfolk, d.o.b. 1900, personal communication, 1988.

45   Mr F.C.W., Wicklewood, Norfolk, d.o.b., 19??, personal communication, 1987.

46   *The Herball or Generall Historie of Plantes*, John Gerarde, The Essence thereof distilled by Marcus Woodward from the Edition of Th. Johnson, 1636, Studio Editions, London, 1985, p. 83.

47   Mr M., Wymondham, Norfolk, d.o.b. 1935, personal communication, 1987.

48   Grieve, *Modern Herbal, op. cit.*, p. 442.

49   *Ibid.*, p. 393.

50   *British Herbal Pharmacopoeia*, British Herbal Medicine Association, 1974, p. 62.

51   *U.S. Dispensatory* 25, 1623.

52   Grieve, *Modern Herbal, op. cit.*, p. 179.

53   Mr J.B., Essex, d.o.b. c.1915, unpublished essay for Age Concern.

54   Mrs C., Whissonsett, Norfolk, d.o.b. c.1920, personal communication, 1988.

55   Mr and Mrs G., Hemsby, Norfolk, d.o.b. c.1930, personal communication, 1988.

56   Mr E.A., South Walsham, Norfolk, personal communication, 1976.

57   Grieve, *Modern Herbal, op. cit.*, p. 839.

58   *British Herball Pharmacopoeia*, see 50, p. 233.

59   Farnsworth, 1968, Lloydia, 246.

60   Mrs H., Swannington, Norfolk, d.o.b. c.1930, personal communication, 1987.

61   *Kitchen Book of Gunton Household*, in Church of St Peter Mancroft, Norwich.

62   *Gunton Household Book*, see 61.

63   Mr and Mrs C., Coltishall, Norfolk, personal communication, 1989.

64   Mrs E.L.J., d.o.b. 1912, unpublished essay for Age Concern, Braintree, Essex.

65   Mr J.B., Colchester, d.o.b. c.1915, unpublished essay for Age Concern.

66   Mrs M., St Osyth, Essex, d.o.b. 1917, unpublished essay for Age Concern.

67   Mrs D.P., Essex, d.o.b. 1900, personal communication, 1989.

68   Mrs E.L.J., d.o.b. 1912, unpublished essay for Age Concern, Braintree, Essex.

69   Mrs A.K., personal communication, 1988.

70   George Baldry, *The Rabbit Skin Cap*, ed. Lilias Rider Haggard, Collins, 1950, p. 209.

71   Mrs D., Horning, Norfolk, personal communication, 1989.

72   Essay for Age Concern, from Brentwood, Essex, 1990. Average age of informants, 80 years.

73   Kenninghall Primary School, Norfolk, 1988.

74   Mrs M.C., West Runton, Norfolk, notebook written by her mother, c.1920.

75   Terrington St Clement Primary School, Norfolk, 1988.

76   Mrs A.E., Whissonsett, Norfolk, d.o.b. c.1945, personal communication, 1988.

77   *British Herbal Pharmacopoeia*, see 46, p. 118.

78   Mrs W.B., Loughton, Essex, d.o.b. 1898, unpublished essay for Age Concern.

79   Mrs E.L.A., Billericay, Essex, d.o.b. 1915, unpublished essay for Age Concern.

80   Mr A.A., Trunch, Norfolk, d.o.b. c.1910, personal communication, 1988.

81   Mrs F.S., Cley, Norfolk, d.o.b. 1920, personal communication, 1988.

82   Kenninghall Primary School, Norfolk, 1988.

83   Mrs A.E., Whissonsett, Norfolk, d.o.b. c.1945, personal communication, 1988.

84   Mrs E.J., Salhouse, Norfolk, d.o.b. 1907, personal communication, 1988.

85   Mr B., Horning, Norfolk, d.o.b. c.1905, personal communication, 1989.

86   Mrs W., Colchester, Essex, d.o.b. c.1920, personal communication, 1988.

87   Mr E.J.C., Wickford, Essex, Age Concern essay, 1990.

88   Sculthorpe Primary School, Norfolk, 1988.

89   Mr E.P., Witton, Norfolk, d.o.b. c.1910, personal communication, 1987.

90   Mr J.A.L., Norwich, d.o.b. c.1930, personal communication, 1987.

91   Mrs S.I., Kenninghall, Norfolk, d.o.b. c.1940, personal communication, 1988.

92   Mr F.C.W., Wicklewood, Norfolk, d.o.b c.1910, personal communication, 1989.

93   Mrs I.H., Flordon Common, Norfolk, d.o.b c.1910, personal communication, 1988.

94   Potter, see (33), p. 194.

95   Terrington St Clement School, Norfolk, 1988.

96   Mrs J., Pedham, Norfolk, d.o.b. c.1930, personal communication, 1988.

97   *I Walked by Night*, see (26) above, page 16.

98   Mrs E.M., Hutton Village, Essex, unpublished essay for Age Concern, 1990.

99   Potter, see (33), p. 124.

100 J. Britten & R. Holland, *Dictionary of English Plant Names*, Trübner, 1878, p. 423.

101 Mr C., Boxted, Essex, d.o.b. 1926, unpublished Age Concern essay.

102 Mrs D., Horning, Norfolk, d.o.b. c.1910, personal communication, 1988.

103 Mrs D.P., Essex, d.o.b. 1900, personal communication, 1989.

104 Mr G., Brundall, d.o.b. c.1920, personal communication, 1989.

105 Mrs M.B., Great Yarmouth, Norfolk, d.o.b. c.1930, personal communication, 1988.

106 Mrs G., Hemsby, Norfolk, d.o.b. c.1930, personal communication, 1988.

107 George Ewart Evans, *The Pattern Under The Plough*, Faber & Faber, 1966, p. 90.

108 J. Britten and R. Holland, *Dictionary of English Plant Names*, 1878, pp. 72 and 149.

109 King's Lynn School, Norfolk, 1988.

110 Mary Chamberlain, *Old Wives Tales*, Virago, 1981.

111 Mr A.C., Hoxne, Suffolk, d.o.b. c.1920, personal communication, 1988.

112 Mundford School, Norfolk, 1986.

113 Enid Porter, *The Folklore of East Anglia*, Batsford 1974, p. 43.

114 Mrs A.A., North Walsham, Norfolk, personal communication, 1988.

115 Chandler, R.F. *et al.*, 1982, *Econ. Bot.* 36 (2), 203.

116 Mrs E.M., St Osyth, Essex, unpublished essay for Age Concern, 1990.

117 Mrs W., Stanton, Suffolk, d.o.b. c.1960, personal communication, 1987.

118 *The Herball or Generall Historie of Plantes*, John Gerarde, the Essence thereof distilled by Marcus Woodward from the Edition of Th. Johnson, 1636, Studio Editions, London, 1985, p. 238.

119 Mrs E.R., Quy, Cambs., d.o.b. c.1920, personal communication, 1987.

120 Mrs M., St Osyth, Essex, d.o.b. 1917, unpublished essay for Age Concern.

121 J. Britten & R. Holland, *op. cit.*, p. 248.

122 Emerson, *Pictures of East Anglian Life*, 1887, p. 91.

123 *British Herbal Pharmacopoeia*, see (46), p. 175.

124 Mrs M. Grieve, *A Modern Herbal*, ed. C.M. Leyel, Capem 1931, p. 596.

125 Mrs S.I., Kenninghall, Norfolk, d.o.b. c.1940, personal communication, 1988.

126 Grieve, *op. cit.*, p. 627.

127 Terrington St Clement School, Norfolk, 1988.

128 *Potter's New Cyclopaedia of Botanical Drugs and Preparations*, R.C. Wren, re-written by Williamson & Evans, 1988, C.W. Daniel Co. Ltd, p. 240.

129 Grieve, *op. cit.*, p. 777.

130 Mrs P., Sheringham, Norfolk, d.o.b. c.1905, personal communication, 1988.

131 Mr A.A., Trunch, Norfolk, d.o.b. c.1910, personal communication, 1988.

132 Potter, *op. cit.*, p. 205.

133 Bircham Women's Institute, Norfolk, personal communication, 1989.

134 Mrs S.I., Kenninghall, Norfolk, d.o.b. c.1940, personal communication, 1988.

135 Mrs B.D.B., Southend, Essex, d.o.b. 1911, unpublished essay for Age Concern, 1990.

136 Potter, *op. cit.*, p. 223.

137 Grieve, *op. cit.*, p. 179.

138 Mrs E.J., Salhouse, Norfolk, d.o.b. 1907, personal communication, 1988.

139 Mr C., Norton Subcourse, Norfolk, d.o.b. c.1920, personal communication, 1989.

140 Mrs J., Pedham, Norfolk, d.o.b. c.1930, personal communication, 1988.

141 Toftwood School, Norfolk, 1988.

142 Miss N., Mundesley, Norfolk, d.o.b. c.1915, personal communication, 1987.

143 Mrs A.E., Whissonsett, Norfolk, d.o.b. c.1945, personal communication, 1988.

144 Mrs D.P., Essex, d.o.b. 1900, personal communication, 1989.

145 Gerarde, *op. cit.*, p. 200.

146 Mrs W.R.R., Colchester, Essex, d.o.b. 1911, unpublished essay for Age Concern.

147 *Gunton Household Book*, Church of St Peter Mancroft, Norwich.

148 Gerarde, *op. cit.*, p. 166.

149 John Pechey, *The Compleat Herbal of Physical Plants*, London, 1694, p. 22.

150 Gerarde, *op. cit.*, p. 273.

151 Pechey, *op. cit.*, p. 159.

152 Mrs H., Swannington, Norfolk, d.o.b. c.1930, personal communication, 1987.

153 Mrs F.S., Cley, Norfolk, d.o.b. 1920, personal communication, 1988.

154 Mrs A.A., North Walsham, Norfolk, d.o.b. c.1940, personal communication, 1988.

155 Miss N., Mundesley, Norfolk, d.o.b. c.1915, personal communication, 1987.

156 Grieve, *op. cit.*, p. 410.

157 Mr J., Lincs., personal communication, 1989.

158 Potter, see (33), p. 283.

159 Mr G.B., Gt Plumstead, Norfolk, d.o.b. c.1910, personal communication, 1989.

160 Mrs A.E., Whissonsett, Norfolk, d.o.b. c.1945, personal communication, 1988.

161 Mrs P., Wicklewood, Norfolk, d.o.b. c.1940, personal communication, 1987.

162 Johnson, E.S. *et al.*, *British Medical Journal*, pp. 291 and 569.

163 Mr J.B., Essex, unpublished Age Concern essay, 1990.

164 Grieve, see (12), p. 806.

165 Mrs H.C., Whissonsett, Norfolk, d.o.b. c.1940, personal communication, 1988.

166 *New Scientist*, 1989, 1687, p. 37.

167 Mrs D.T., Rockland St Mary, Norfolk, d.o.b. c.1910, personal communication, 1989.

168 Potter, *op. cit.*, p. 93.

169 Mr J.B., Essex, Age Concern essay.

170 Grieve, *op. cit.*, p. 641.

171 Potter, *op. cit.*, p. 219.
172 B.J. and H.L.B., Heacham, Norfolk.
173 *British Herbal Pharmacopoeia*, British Herbal Medicine Association, 1974, p. 41.
174 Potter, *op. cit.*, p. 93.
175 Mrs V., Bocking, Essex.
176 Grieve, *op. cit.*, p. 763.
177 *Op. cit.*, p. 63.
178 John Pechey, *op. cit.*, p. 63.
179 *British Herbal Pharmacopoeia*, *op. cit.*, p. 62.
180 Mrs S.I., Kenninghall, Norfolk, d.o.b. c.1940, personal communication, 1988.
181 Quoted in Grieve, *op. cit.*, p. 14.
182 Mrs T., Cambs.
183 Mrs S.B., Norwich.
184 Mrs M.S., Braintree, Essex, d.o.b. c.1940, personal communication, 1988.
185 Mr J.B., Colchester, Essex, Age Concern essay.
186 Mrs S.I. Kenninghall, Norfolk, d.o.b. c.1940, personal communication, 1988.
187 Potter, *op. cit.*, p. 290.
188 Mrs P.B., Norwich, d.o.b. c.1935, personal communication, 1986.
189 Mrs S., Southrepps, Norfolk, d.o.b. c.1945, personal communication, 1986.
190 Mr J.B., Colchester, Essex, Age Concern essay, 1990.
191 Grieve, *op. cit.*, p. 581.
192 Manuscript in private possession, D.K., Ipswich.
193 Mr D.E.B., Chelmsford, Essex, d.o.b. 1925, Age Concern essay.
194 *British Pharmaceutical Codex*, 1923, p. 957.
195 *I Walked by Night*, ed. Lilias Rider Haggard, Boydell Press, 1974, p. 16.
196 Miss N., Mundesley, Norfolk, d.o.b. c.1915, personal communication, 1987.
197 Kenninghall School, Norfolk, 1988.
198 Elizabeth Harland, *No Halt at Sunset*, Benn.
199 Mrs A.R., Norwich, d.o.b. c.1935, personal communication, 1989.
200 Mr F.C.W., Wicklewood, Norfolk, d.o.b. c.1920, personal communication, 1988.
201 King's Lynn School, Norfolk, 1988.
202 Mrs A.A., North Walsham, Norfolk, d.o.b. c.1940, personal communication, 1988.
203 Docking School, Norfolk, 1988.
204 Mr G.H. d.o.b. 1900, personal communication, 1987.
205 Mr J.B., Colchester, Essex, Age Concern Essay, 1990.
206 *Ibid.*
207 Mrs M., St Osyth, Essex, d.o.b. 1917, Age Concern essay, 1990.
208 Mrs I.H., Flordon Common, Norfolk, d.o.b. c.1920, personal communication, 1988.
209 Mrs L.M.H., Colchester, Essex, Age Concern essay, 1990.
210 Terrington St Clement School, Norfolk, 1988.
211 Grieve, *op. cit.*, p. 777.
212 Mrs L.B., Colchester, Essex, d.o.b. c.1920, personal communication, 1988.
213 Mr R.H., Eriswell, Suffolk, d.o.b. c.1920, personal communication, 1987.
214 Toftwood School, Norfolk, 1988.
215 Logan Home Papers, Scottish Records Office, GDI.384/26.
216 Grieve, *op. cit.*, p. 655.
217 Mrs A.H.S., d.o.b. c.1945, personal communication, 1992.

218 *British Herbal Pharmacopoeia, op. cit.*, p. 148.
219 Miss K.S., Heckington, Lincs.
220 Dr J.M.B., Wrentham, Suffolk.
221 Mr C., Norton Subcourse, Norfolk, d.o.b. c.1920, personal communication, 1989.
222 Pechey, *op. cit.*, p. 139.
223 *Gunton Household Book, op. cit.*
224 Mrs D.B., Tacolneston, Norfolk, d.o.b. c.1935, personal communication, 1988.
225 Mr D.H., Lowestoft, Suffolk, d.o.b. c.1920, personal communication 1988.
226 Mr J.B., Colchester, Essex, Age Concern essay, 1990.
227 Mrs H.E., Norwich, d.o.b. c.1940, personal communication, 1987.
228 Mrs L.M.H., Colchester, Essex, Age Concern essay, 1990.
229 Mr R.C., Norton Subcourse, Norfolk, d.o.b. c.1920, personal communication, 1988.
230 Mrs P.B., Norwich, d.o.b. c.1935, personal communication, 1986.
231 Mrs G.R.F., Loddon, Norfolk, d.o.b. c.1925, personal communication, 1987.
232 Petch and Swann, *Flora of Norfolk*, p. 168.
233 Bircham Women's Institute, Norfolk, 1988.
234 Whissonsett Happy Circle, Norfolk, 1988.
235 Mrs I.H., Flordon Common, Norfolk, d.o.b. c.1920, personal communication, 1988.
236 Grieve, *op. cit.*, p. 196.
237 B.W., Hindolveston, Norfolk, d.o.b. c.1935, personal communication, 1988.
238 Mr R.C., Norton Subcourse, Norfolk, d.o.b. c.1920, personal communication, 1988.
239 Mrs R.L., Norwich, d.o.b. c.1930, personal communication, 1989.
240 Mr D.H., Lowestoft, Suffolk, d.o.b. c.1920, personal communication, 1989.
241 Potter, *op. cit.*, p. 227.
242 Mr F.C.W., Wicklewood, Norfolk, d.o.b. c.1910, personal communication, 1989.
243 Mrs J.B., Age Concern essay, 1990.
244 Mrs L.M.H., Essex, Age Concern essay, 1990.
245 Mr S., Foulsham, Norfolk, d.o.b. c.1920, personal communication 1988.
246 Mr F.C.W., Wicklewood, Norfolk, d.o.b. 1910, personal communication, 1988.
247 Mrs d.P., Essex, d.o.b. 1900, personal communication, 1988.
248 Mrs A.E., Whissonsett, Norfolk, d.o.b. c.1945, personal communication, 1988.
249 Mrs M.B., Gt Yarmouth, Norfolk, d.o.b. c.1930, personal communication, 1988.
250 Mrs M.P., Norwich, Norfolk, d.o.b. c.1940, personal communication, 1987.
251 Kenninghall School, Norfolk, 1988.
252 King's Lynn Primary School, Norfolk, 1988.
253 Grieve, *op. cit.*, p. 571.
254 Mr R.C., Norton Subcourse, Norfolk, d.o.b., c.1920, personal communication, 1989.
255 Mr F.C.W., Wicklewood, Norfolk, d.o.b. c.1910, personal communication, 1988.
256 Mrs M.P., Hoveton, Norfolk, d.o.b. c.1935, personal communication, 1988.
257 Grieve, *op. cit.*, p. 272.
258 Mr J.B., Colchester, Essex, Age Concern essay, 1990.
259 Kenninghall School, Norfolk, 1988.
260 Mr F.C.W., see 156.
261 Gerarde, *op. cit.*, p. 20.
262 Mr L.S., Fundenhall, Norfolk, d.o.b. c.1925, personal communication, 1988.
263 Mrs I.H., Flordon Common, Norfolk, d.o.b. c.1915, personal communication, 1987.
264 Mr A.B., Whissonsett, Norfolk, d.o.b. c.1915, personal communication, 1987.

265 Mundford Primary School, 1988.
266 Mr F.C.W., Wicklewood, Norfolk, d.o.b. c.1910, personal communication, 1988.
267 *Ibid.*
268 Mrs A.H.L., Aylsham, Norfolk, d.o.b. c.1935, personal communication, 1992.
269 Grieve, *op. cit.*, p. 257.
270 Grieve, *op. cit.*, p. 690.
271 Mr J.A.L., Norwich, d.o.b. c.1930, personal communication, 1988.
272 Mr. F.C.W., see note 156.
273 Mrs d.P., Essex, d.o.b. 1900, personal communication, 1988.
274 Grieve, *op. cit.*, p. 315.
275 Mr F.C.W., see note 156.
276 Mrs E.M., Barking, Essex, d.o.b. c.1915, personal communication, 1987.
277 Mr F.C.W., see note 156.
278 Potter, *op. cit.*, p. 32.
279 *Folklore*, 62, 1951, pp. 252–266.
280 *The Poor Man's Physician or the Receits of the Famous John Moncrief of Tippermalloch*, 3rd edn, Edinburgh, 1731, p. 97.
281 Gerarde, *op. cit.*, p. 88.
282 Mr D.H., Lowestoft, Suffolk, d.o.b. c.1920, personal communication, 1988.
283 Mr F.C.W., see note 156.
284 Mr M.M. Wymondham, Norfolk, d.o.b. 1925, personal communication, 1988.
285 Mr J.A.L., Norwich, d.o.b. 1930, personal communication, 1988.
286 Mr D.E.B. Essex, d.o.b. 1925, personal communication, 1988.
287 Mr J.K., Norfolk, d.o.b. c.1930, personal communication, 1987.
288 Bircham WI, Norfolk.
289 F.C.W. Norfolk, personal communication; L.M.H. Essex, personal communication.
290 E.J., Essex, personal communication; Kenninghall School, Norfolk.
291 Alderman Peel School, Norfolk.
292 Mrs E.J., Salhouse, Norfolk, personal communication.
293 M.P., Norwich, personal communication.
294 Terrington St Clement School, Norfolk.
295 Mrs M.D., Norfolk, personal communication.
296 Moncrief, *op. cit.*
297 Grieve, *op. cit.*, p. 312.

CHAPTER THREE

1 George Ewart Evans, *Where Beards Wag All*, Faber & Faber, 1970, p. 18.
2 Henry Bracken, MD, *Farriery Improved*, 1789, p. 68.
3 Mr J.C., Hemblington, Norfolk, personal communication,
4 Ernest R. Suffling, *History and Legends of the Broads District, Jarrold*, 1891, p. 87.
5 Norwich City Library Collection of Notes by Mark R. Taylor, Norfolk Records Office, MS4322, 57 x 1.
6 Anne E. Jones, 'Folk Medicine in Living Memory in Wales', *Folk Life*, 18, 1980, pp. 58–68.
7 Mr D.H., Lowestoft, personal communication

8 Mrs. P.B., Norwich, personal communication.
9 Minutes of Cringleford Women's Institute, 1925.
10 George Ewart Evans, 'Flesh and Blood Archives: Some Early Experiences', *Oral History*, 1, p. 3.
11 Report on Norfolk Schools Survey, ed. Hatfield, in press (Folklore Society).
12 Anne E. Jones, *op. cit.*
13 See for example *Potter's New Cyclopaedia of Botanical Drugs and Preparations*, R.C. Wren, Health Science Press, 1975.
14 Dom Yoder, 'Folk Medicine' in Richard M. Dorson (ed.), *Folklore and Folklife: an Introduction*, Chicago & London, 1972, p. 191.

CHAPTER FOUR

1 Mrs D.T., Rockland St Mary, Norfolk, d.o.b. c.1910, personal communication, 1989.
2 Mr & Mrs S., Foulsham, Norfolk, d.o.b. c.1930, personal communication, 1988.
3 Mrs. J., Salhouse, Norfolk, d.o.b. c.1910, personal communication, 1988.
4 *Potter's, New Cyclopaedia of Botanical Drugs and Preparations*, by R.C. Wren, revised Williamson & Evans, 1988, C.W. Daniel Co. Ltd, Saffron Walden, p. 296.
5 Potter, *op. cit.*, p. 296.
6 Mr A.A., Trunch, Norfolk, d.o.b. c.1915, personal communication, 1989.
7 Anne E. Jones, 'Folk Medicine in Living Memory in Wales', *Folk Life*, (18), 1980, pp. 58–68.
8 L.F. Newman & E.M. Wilson, 'Folk-lore Survivals in the Southern Lake Counties and in Essex: a Comparison and Contrast', Part I, *Folklore*, 1951, 62, pp. 252–266.

CHAPTER FIVE

1 Dom Yoder, 'Folk Medicine' in Richard M. Dorson (ed.), *Folklore and Folklife: An Introduction*, Chicago, 1972, p. 191.
2 E.G. Wheelwright, *The Physick Garden*, Cape, 1934, p. 108.
3 Dr J. Anderson, *The Bee*, vol. VI, Dec. 1791, p. 243.
4 G. Hatfield, Ph.D. thesis, University of Edinburgh, 1980.
5 *Herbal Review*, The Herb Society, summer 1978, pp. 15–20.
6 Barbara Griggs, *Green Pharmacy: A History of Herbal Medicine*, 1981, Jill Norman & Hobhouse Ltd.
7 Mr E.J.C., Wickford, Essex, d.o.b. 1925, Age Concern essay, 1991.
8 Quoted in Jacques Rousseau, 'Essays in Biohistory', *International Association for Plant Taxonomy*, Dec. 1970, Utrecht, Netherlands, p. 195.
9 Mrs E.M., St Osyth, Essex, d.o.b. 1917, Age Concern essay, 1991.
10 S.G. Harrison, *et al.*, *The Oxford Book of Food Plants*, London, 1985, p. 14.
11 Mr G.G., Hoxne, Suffolk, personal communication, 1989.
12 Mrs I.P., Hoxne, Suffolk, personal communication, 1989.
13 Mr S., Whissonett, Norfolk, d.o.b. c.1915, personal communication, 1989.
14 Mrs. L.C., Pulham St Mary, Norfolk, d.o.b. c.1930, personal communication, 1990.
15 *Potter's New Cyclopaedia of Botanical Drugs and Preparations*, R.C. Wren, re-written Williamson & Evans, C.W. Daniel, Saffron Walden, 1988, p. 79.
16 Mrs H.S., Foulsham, Norfolk, d.o.b. c.1930, personal communication, 1988.

17   Mrs W.S., Stanton, Suffolk, d.o.b. c.1955, personal communication, 1988.

18   Mrs S.I., near Kenninghall, Norfolk, d.o.b. c.1940, personal communication, 1988.

19   *British Pharmaceutical Codex*, British Pharmaceutical Press, 1923, p. 909.

20   Potter, *op. cit.*, p. 229.

21   Leslie F. Newman, 'Some Notes on the Pharmacology and Therapeutic Value of Folk-Medicines', I, *Folk Lore* 59, Sept. 1948, p. 119.

22   John Pechey, *The Compleat Herbal of Physical Plants*, London, 1694, p. 81.

23   E.S. Johnson, *et al.*, 1985, *British Medical Journal*, 291, 569. Also D.M. Hylands & P. Hylands, 1986, *Abstract of the Phytochemical Society European Meeting, Lausanne, 3–5th September, 1986*, p. 17.

24   See note 9.

25   Mrs C., Hoxne, Suffolk, d.o.b. c.1940, personal communication, 1988.

26   *Potter's New Cyclopaedia of Botanical Drugs and Preparations*, by R.C. Wren, 1975 edition, Health Science Press, p. 206.

27   John Pechey, *op. cit.*, p. 130.

28   David Hoffman, *The Holistic Herbal*, Findhorn Press, 1983, p. 209.

29   Mrs d.W., Colchester, Essex, d.o.b. c.1945, personal communication, 1990.

30   *The Olio Cookery Book* by L. Sykes, Ernest Benn, London, 1928, p. 237.

31   *Ibid.*, p. 239.

32   *Ibid.*, p. 238.

33   *Ibid.*, p. 244.

34   *Ibid.*, p. 247.

35   *The Woman's Treasury for Home and Garden*, ed. MacSelf, London, Amateur Gardening Offices, n.d., p. 292–294.

CHAPTER SIX

1   Mrs M.W., Saffron Walden, Essex, d.o.b. 1920, Age Concern essay, 1991.

2   Peter W. Nolan, 'Folk Medicine in Rural Ireland', *Folk Life*, 27, 1988–9, pp. 44–56.

3   Quoted in Mrs C.F. Leyel, *The Magic of Herbs*, Jonathan Cape, London, 1926, p. 253.

4   Letter in *Folklore and Customs of Rural England*, by Margaret Baker, David and Charles, 1974, pp. 169–170.

5   Letter to Dr Taylor from Dr James of Fressingfield, Suffolk, among Taylor's notes.

6   Mr D.E.B., Boreham, Essex, d.o.b. 1925, Age Concern essay, 1991.

7   Leslie F. Newman, 'Some Notes on the Pharmacology and Therapeutic Value of Folk-Medicine', *Folk Lore*, Sept. 1948, LIX, pp. 118–135.

8   *Gunton Household Book*, MS in Church of St Peter Mancroft, Norwich, p. 24.

9   Mrs E.M., St Osyth, Essex, d.o.b. 1917, Age Concern essay, 1991.

10   Mrs P.B., Norwich, personal communication, 1986.

11   Mr L.C., Pulham St Mary, Norfolk, personal communication, 1977.

12   Mr J.F., Earlham, Norwich, personal communication, 1988.

13   Ms C.M., Norwich, personal communication, 1988.

14   E.S. Johnson, *et al.*, *British Medical Journal*, 1985, 291, pp. 569–573.

15   *Chemistry in Britain*, 23, 1987, p. 100.

16   *New Scientist*, 1684, 1989, p. 32.

17   *Diabetes Care*, vol. 1, no. 2, 1992, pp. 10–11.

APPENDIX: SUMMARY TABLE OF RECORDED PLANT REMEDIES, WITH SOURCES

Name of Plant	Remedy	Recorded by Taylor, 1920	Recorded by Hatfield 1990
Agrimony (Agrimonia eupatoria L.)	Dried and infused for lumbago and rheumatism		E. Harland, d.o.b. 1951
	Made into ointment for wounds in horses and cattle		F.C.W., Wicklewood, Norfolk d.o.b. c.1910
	Decoction for jaundice, diabetes dropsy, burns		F.C.W.
	Shoots brewed for jaundice	For liver disease (no source given)	Mrs S.I. Kenninghall, Norfolk d.o.b. c.1940
Alkanet (Alkanna tinctoria (L.) Tausch	Decoction in wine makes a good ointment		F.C.W. Norfolk
Apple (Malus sp)	Rotten apple rubbed on to 'any sore place'		Mr S., Norfolk d.o.b. c.1930
Balm (Melissa officinalis L.)	For colds and fevers		Miss G. Artleborough
Barley (Hordeum distichon L.)	Boiled barley gives strength and prevents hair greying		Mr D., Walcott d.o.b. c.1920
Birch (Betula sp)	'Turpentine' from birch bark use to oil horses hooves		Mr M.C., Norfolk d.o.b. c.1940

Name of Plant	Remedy	Recorded by Taylor, 1920	Recorded by Hatfield 1990
Bird's eye, 'sore eyes' (*Veronica sp*)	Infusion of flowers for sore eyes		Mrs A.E., Norfolk d.o.b. c.1945
Bistort (*Polygonum bistorta L.*)	Juice from leaves rubbed round horses' teeth to prevent decay		F.C.W., Norfolk d.o.b. c.1910
Bladder-wrack (*Fucus vesiculosus L.*)	Slime from bladders used in bath to ease arthritis		Mrs A.E., Norfolk d.o.b. c.1940
Bramble (*Rubus fruticosus agg.*)	For thrush in horses	Baconsthorpe WI	
	As a poultice for cancer	Huntingfield WI	
	Leaves for diarrhoea		Mrs W., Colchester d.o.b. c.1945
	Leaves fed to rabbits for pod belly		Mr G., Hemsby d.o.b. c.1930
	Leaves boiled with honey, water, allum and white wine for teeth		Mr F.C.W., Norfolk d.o.b. c.1910
Broad bean	Furry inside of pod rubbed on to warts	Mrs S. Butler	Numberous records, e.g. Mrs E., Norwich
	Inhale perfume of flowers for whooping cough	Sproughton WI	Terrington St Clement Sch.
	Root used as liniment or compress	Ashby WI	
Bryony (*Bryonia dioica Jacq.*)	Root roasted and grated, fed to horses as tonic		Mr. C., Norfolk d.o.b. 1935

Name of Plant	Remedy	Recorded by Taylor, 1920	Recorded by Hatfield 1990
Buckbean (*Menyanthes trifoliata L.*) Bulfer, puffball (*Lycoperdon sp*)	Decoction of seed for rheumatism	'Bird'	
	Dust for cuts To stop bleeding from varicose veins	EDP 1905	Mr G. and other Mrs M.B. Gt Yarmouth d.o.b. c.1940
	Chopped and made into poultice for carbuncles		Hoxne Circle Suffolk
Cabbage (*Brassica oleracea*)	Poultice for boils	Blythburgh WI	Terrington St Clement Sch.
	Cabbage water 'purifies blood' Outer leaves boiled – drink water for rheumatism		Lion's Centre, Essex Mr L.M.H., Essex d.o.b. c.1930
Celery (*Apium graveolens*)	Leaves cooked in lard for sores and ulcers	Mrs S.B.	
	Infusion of seed for Rheumatism	Cringleford WI	Kenninghall School
	Chew for relief of hangover		Mr G.B., Norfolk d.o.b. c.1915

Name of Plant	Remedy	Recorded by Taylor, 1920	Recorded by Hatfield 1990
Chamomile (*Chamaemelum nobile L.*)	Tea for a cold Tea for constipation Infusion of flowers for sore eyes Oil for psoriasis	Eyke WI	Terrington St Clement Sch Toftwood Sch Happy Circle Hoxne, Suffolk
Chickweed (*Stellaria media Vill*)	Boiled for poultices Boiled and applied to boils Poultice for eczema and dermatitus Fed to chickens for 'gapes'	Miss G., Attleborough	Mrs F.S., Norfolk d.o.b. c.1920 Mr R.C., Norfolk d.o.b. c.1930 d.o.b. 1935
Chicory (*Cichorium intybus L.*)	Dried and infused for lumbago and Rheumatism		Mrs E.H., Norfolk d.o.b. c.1910
Cloves (*Syzygium aromaticum (L.) Merr. et Perry*)	Soaked for constipation	Huntingfield WI	
Coltsfoot (*Tussilago farfara L.*)	Infusion of leaves or root for coughs Flowers and leaves dried and smoked for coughs		Kenninghall Sch. & others Several records e.g. Mrs J., Norfolk, d.o.b. c.1910

Name of Plant	Remedy	Recorded by Taylor, 1920	Recorded by Hatfield 1990
Comfrey (*Symphytum officinale L.*)	With louseleek and marshmallow for inflammation	Dr B., Lincoln	
	Poultice from roots for broken wrists		Miss S., Norfolk d.o.b. c.1900
	Fed to horses, geese, chickens as tonic		Mrs I.H., Norfolk d.o.b. c.1930
	Infused for rheumatism		Mr G.R., Suffolk d.o.b. c.1920
	Root chewed for sore throat		Mr E.P., Norfolk d.o.b. c.1905
	Tea as tonic and good for blood		Mr F.W., Norfolk d.o.b. c.1910
	Ointment from roots for sprains and open wounds		Several records e.g. Kenninghall Sch.
	Ointment from leaves for bruises		Mrs. S.I., Norfolk d.o.b. c.1940
	Ointment from roots for leg ulcers		Mrs S.I., Norfolk d.o.b. c.1940
Cornflower (*Centaurea cyanus L.*)	With chamomile and rose, compress for tired eyes		Mrs. R., Essex d.o.b. 1911

Name of Plant	Remedy	Recorded by Taylor, 1920	Recorded by Hatfield 1990
Couch grass, foul grass (*Agropyron repens (L.) Beauv.*)	Infusion of rhizomes for stones in gall bladder, kidneys Infusion of rhizomes for uriniary troubles		Mr F.W., Norfolk d.o.b. c.1910 Several records e.g. Mr J.B., Essex d.o.b. c.1920
Cow parsley (*Anthriscus sylvestris (L.) Hoffm.*)	Hot infusion of cow parsley and elder leaves to treat laminitis in ponies; leaves also fed		Miss N., Norfolk d.o.b. c.1920
Crowfoot (*Ranunculus sp*)	Juice from stalks dropped onto warts		Terrington St Clement Sch.
Cuckoo flower, lady's smock (*Cardamine pratensis L.*)	Leaves as diuretic for animals		Mr F.W., Norfolk d.o.b. c.1910
Cucumber (*Cucumis sativus*)	Good for skin and eyes Laid in cot to allay fever in child		Mrs J., Norfolk d.o.b. c.1910 Mr F.W., Norfolk d.o.b. c.1910
Currant (*Ribes nigrum*)	Infusion of leaves as a gargle Boiled with haryhound and dandelion to make spring medicine Tea or syrup made from blackcurrants for colds	Huntingfield WI Miss G. Artleborough	Several records e.g. Mrs P., Norfolk d.o.b. c.1930

Name of Plant	Remedy	Recorded by Taylor, 1920	Recorded by Hatfield 1990
Currant (*cont.*)	Leaves macerated, liquid used for gout and fevers		Mr F.W., Norfolk d.o.b. c.1910
Dandelion (*Taracacum officinale Weber*)	Infusion for indigestion	Wilby WI	
	Tea for 'spring humours'	Mr J. Rochford	
	Infusion of flowers for cough		Mrs P., Norfolk d.o.b. c.1900
			Whissonsett Circle
	Juice used to remove cancer on lip		Mrs P., Norwich d.o.b. c.1930
	Juice used for warts		Mr M., Norfolk d.o.b. c.1930
	Leaves chewed for arthritis		Mrs R., Norwich d.o.b. c.1930
	Infusion of leaves applied for eczema		Mr J.B., Essex d.o.b. c.1925
	Roots used to purify blood and restore appetite		
Deadly nightshade (*Atropa belladonna L.*)	Juice mixed with lard for chilblains		Mr J.B., Essex d.o.b. c.1925
Dock (*Rumex sp*)	Poultice for cancer	Baconsthorpe WI	
	Root boiled and mixed with lard for shingles and eczema	Mr V. Bocking	
	Leaves on brow for headache		Mrs H., Norfolk d.o.b. c.1900

Name of Plant	Remedy	Recorded by Taylor, 1920	Recorded by Hatfield 1990
Dock (*cont.*)	Leaves chewed as tonic		Mr M., Norfolk d.o.b. c.1930
	Leaves wrapped round chapped thighs in winter		Mr H., Suffolk d.o.b. c.1920
	For greasy fetlocks in shire horses, wrap overnight in large dock leaves		Mr H., Suffolk d.o.b. c.1920
	Ripe seed boiled and liquid drunk for drawing wound or boil		Mr D.B., Essex d.o.b. c.1925
	Leaf treated with brandy and applied to cuts		Mr D.C., Essex d.o.b. 1926
	Roots ground into cures for blood disorders		Mr J.B., Essex d.o.b. c.1920
Elder (*Sambucus nigra L.*)	Mixed with peppermint for appendicitis		Wilby WI
	Shoots boiled for eczema	Cringleford WI	
	Green leaves rubbed onto eczema, infusion of flowers ditto		Mrs E.H., Norfolk d.o.b. c.1910
	Hot berry wine for a cold	Eyke WI	Numerous records e.g. Mrs A., Norfolk d.o.b. 1900
	Ointment from flowers for ulcers and sore feet	Dr T, Oulton Broad	

Name of Plant	Remedy	Recorded by Taylor, 1920	Recorded by Hatfield 1990
Elder (*cont.*)	Flower ointment for rough hands and grazes		Mrs H.E., Norfolk d.o.b. c.1930
	Flower ointment for slow-healing wounds		Mr M.G.R., Suffolk d.o.b. c.1920
	Skin ointment made from inner bark, leaves and flowers		Mr J.B., Essex d.o.b. c.1920
	For foot-rot in sheep	Baconsthorpe WI	
	Leaves with suet for gout		Mr F.C.W., Norfolk d.o.b. c.1910
	Stem rubbed onto warts		King's lynn Sch.
'Elicampain' elecampane (*Inula helenium L.*)	Roots dried and grated with sugar for coughs	Huntingfield WI	
Eyebright (*Euphrasia officinalis L.*)	Infusion for sore eyes		Miss N., Norfolk d.o.b. c.1920
Feverfew (*Tanacetum parthenium (L.) Schultz Bip*)	Poultice for toothache	Orford WI	
	Infusion for coughs		Mrs F.S., Norfolk d.o.b. c.1920
	For migraine		Several records e.g. Mr R., Suffolk d.o.b. c.1910
	For arthritis		Several records e.g. Docking Sch.

Name of Plant	Remedy	Recorded by Taylor, 1920	Recorded by Hatfield 1990
Feverfew (*cont.*)	Infusion for hot flushes during menopause		Hoxne Circle Suffolk
Fig (*Ficus caria L.*)	Juice of leaf for warts		Mrs J., Norfolk d.o.b. c.1910
Figwort 'bruff betony' (*Scrophularia nodosa L.*)	For teething in children		Mrs D.P., Essex d.o.b. c.1900
Fir (*Abies sp*)	Resin chewed to keep heart healthy		Mr R.C., Norfolk d.o.b. c.1920
Geranium sp	Bruised leaves for cuts		King's Lynn Sch.
Goosegrass (*Galium aparine L.*)	Infusion to bathe cuts		Mr F, Norfolk d.o.b. c.1950 Mrs M., Essex d.o.b. 1907
	Lotion for ringworm in dogs		Miss N., Norfolk d.o.b. c.1920
	Made into 'beer' with nettles and ginger to clear blood		Mr D.B., Essex d.o.d. 1925
Greater celandine (*Chelidonium majus L.*)	Juice painted on warts	Mrs B., Norwich	Several records e.g. Kenninghall Sch.

Name of Plant	Remedy	Recorded by Taylor, 1920	Recorded by Hatfield 1990
Ground elder (*Aegopodium podagraria L.*)	Fed to ill sow		Mr T.R., Norfolk d.o.b. c.1925
	Young shoots eaten for gout		Mr F.C.W., Norfolk d.o.b. c.1910
	Made into ointment with comfrey for cuts and grazes		Mrs S.W., Suffolk d.o.b. c.1955
	Boil shoots, use liquid to treat piles		Mr D.B., Essex d.o.b. 1925
Ground ivy	Infusion for colds	Wilby WI	
	Infusion to bathe sore eyes		Mrs D.P., Essex d.o.b. c.1900
	With celandine, daisies, sugar and rose water for sore eyes		Mr F.C.W., Norfolk d.o.b. c.1910
Groundsel 'secention' (*Senecio vulgaris L.*)	Poultice for boils	Eyke WI	Mrs S., Norfolk d.o.b. c.1930 and Mr R., Norfolk d.o.b. c.1900
	Hot poultice for quinsy in horses		Mr D.H., Suffolk d.o.b. c.1920
	Softened in milk to relieve teething pains in babies		Mr F.C.W., Norfolk d.o.b. c.1910

Name of Plant	Remedy	Recorded by Taylor, 1920	Recorded by Hatfield 1990
Heal-all tree 'ee-law' (*Sedum rosea*)	One side of leaf to heal cuts, other side to draw puss	Blythburgh WI	Mrs E.R., Cambs. d.o.b. c.1920 Mrs M., Essex d.o.b. 1917
Heartsease (*Viola tricolor L.*)	Taken in white wine, good for heart		Mr F.C.W., Norfolk d.o.b. c.1910
Hedge garlic (*Alliaria petiolata* (Bieb) *Cavara & Grande*)	Chewed for sore gums and mouth ulcers Made into ointment for bruises etc.		Mrs A.E., Norfolk d.o.b. c.1945 Mrs D.P., Essex d.o.b. c.1900
Hedge woundwort (*Stachys sylvatica L.*)	Poultice of leaves for boils and carbuncles		Mrs M.S., Essex d.o.b. 1914
Hemlock (*Conium maculatum L.*)	To stimulate horse's appetite Dried, powered, put on cuts to stop bleeding	Dr H.	Hoxne Circle, Essex
Henbane (*Hyoscyamus niger L.*)	Root soaked in vinegar for toothache		Mr F.C.W., Norfolk d.o.b. c.1910
Holly (*Ilex aquifolium L.*)	Beat chilblains with holly till they bleed		Several records, e.g. Mrs J., Essex d.o.b. c.1930

Name of Plant	Remedy	Recorded by Taylor, 1920	Recorded by Hatfield 1990
Holly (*cont.*)	Holly berries powdered mixed with lard as chilblain ointment		Mr J.B., Essex d.o.b. c.1935
Honeysuckle	Infusion of flowers for headache Inhalation for asthma		Miss N., Norfolk d.o.b. c.1920
Horehound 'harehound' 'hary hound' (*Marrubium vulgare L.*)	To promote appetite For a cold 'Beer' for coughs	Miss G. Wilby WI	Mrs H., Norfolk d.o.b. c.1900
	In wine for coughs and colds		Mr F.C.W., Norfolk d.o.b. c.1910 and Kenninghall Sch.
Horse chestnut (*Aesculus hippocastanum*)	Necklace of conkers worn to prevent rheumatism		Mundford School
Horse pepper (*Angelica archangelica L.*)	Young shoots eaten as tonic		Mr D.H., Suffolk d.o.b. c.1920
	For rheumatics		Mr F.C.W., Norfolk d.o.b. c.1910
Horseradish (*Armoracia rusticana* (*Gaertn*) *May & Scherb*)	Juice in which root has been boiled for coughs For catarrh		Mr B., Norfolk d.o.b. c.1905 Mrs D.W., Essex d.o.b. c.1935

Name of Plant	Remedy	Recorded by Taylor, 1920	Recorded by Hatfield 1990
Horseradish (*cont.*)	Root grated and soaked, applied as poultice for lumbago		Mr J.B., Essex d.o.b. c.1935
	Applied to bad cut		Mundford School
Houseleek (*Sempervivum tectorum L.*)	Juice for insect bites, stings, vaccinations	Miss S., Lincs	
	As poultice for bad breasts	Ancaster, lincs	
	Infusion for croup	Dr N., Suffolk	
	For shingles and eczema	Mr V., Bocking	
	Mixed with comfrey and marshmallow for inflamation	Dr B., Lincoln	
	Ointment for a sore		
	Infusion for Asthma	Huntingfield WI	
	Juice to keep skin clear		Mr J., Lincs d.o.b. c.1950
			Mrs A., Norfolk d.o.b. c.1940
			Mrs D., Norfolk d.o.b. c.1920
	Rubbed on warts		Mrs D., Norfolk d.o.b. c.1920
	Leaves for cuts		Mrs F.S., Norfolk d.o.b. c.1920
	Juice in ear for earache		Numberous records e.g. Kenninghall Sch.

Name of Plant	Remedy	Recorded by Taylor, 1920	Recorded by Hatfield 1990
Houseleek (*cont.*)	Juice squeezed into child's eyes for conjunctivitis		Mrs M.J., Norfolk d.o.b. c.1935
	For sores and skin infections		Mr F.C.W., Norfolk d.o.b. c.1910
	Juice for chapped lips		Mr J.B., Essex d.o.b. c.1935
	Poultice for cancerous growths		Mr J.B., Essex d.o.b. c.1935
	Poultice for boils, abscesses		Mundford School
	For freckles		Mundford School
	For sore feet		Mundford School
	Infusion for stomach ache		Mundford School
Iris sp	Decoction of root, with oak apples, vinegar, sulphur, as ointment for spots and skin complaints		Mr F.C.W., Norfolk d.o.b. c.1910
Ivy (*Hedera helix L.*)	Fed to stock for expulsion of afterbirth	Dr H.	Mr A., Norfolk d.o.b. c.1920 several other records
	Leaves in vinegar for bunions	Ancaster, Lincs.	
	For ulcers and sore feet	Dr T., Oulton Broad	
	Bruise leaf and stick on corn		Mr C., Norfolk d.o.b. c.1930

Name of Plant	Remedy	Recorded by Taylor, 1920	Recorded by Hatfield 1990
Ivy (*cont.*)	Fed to cows, goats, horses for loss of appetite		Several records e.g. Mrs I.H., Norfolk d.o.b. c.1930
	Leaves with oil and vinegar for burns		Mr M., Norfolk d.o.b. c.1930
Juniper (*Juniperus sp*)	Abortion	Mrs S.B., Norwich	
	Rheumatism	Mrs S.B., Norwich	
	Oil for low back pain in man and horse		Miss N., Norfolk d.o.b. c.1029
Lavender (*Lavendula sp*)	Burnt in sick-room and used as antiseptic		Mrs A., Norfolk d.o.b. c.1940
Less celandine (*Ranunculus ficaria L.*)	Decoction for liver cancer	Dr B., Lowestoft	
	For piles	Mr W., Mattishall	Mr J.B., Essex d.o.b. c.1935
	Leaves and flowers made into ointment for any sore place		Mrs D.P., Essex d.o.b. c.1900
Lettuce (*Lactuca sativa*)	For sleeplessness	Ashby WI	
Lime tree (*Tilia sp*)	Infusion of flowers for headache		Mrs A., Norfolk d.o.b. c.1040

Name of Plant	Remedy	Recorded by Taylor, 1920	Recorded by Hatfield 1990
Linseed (*Linum usitatissimum L.*)	Boiled for poulticing man and beast		*Miss N., Norfolk d.o.b. c.1920*
	Fed to horses to increase bloom on coat		Mr F., Norfolk d.o.b. c.1935
	Hot poultice for quinsy in horses		Mr D.H., Suffolk d.o.b. c.1920
	With cold bran for coughs in animals		Mr F.C.W., Norfolk d.o.b. c.1910
	With cream of tartar and treacle for strangles in horses		Mr F.C.W., Norfolk d.o.b. c.1910
	Poultice for housemaid's knee		Mr J.B., Essex d.o.b. c.1935
Lobelia (*Lobelia inflata L.*)	For asthma		King's Lynn Sch.
Mallow 'pick cheese' (*Malva sylvestris L.*)	Fruit chewed as a laxative		Mrs E., Norfolk d.o.b. c.1950
	Shoots made into poultice for boils		Several records e.g. Mrs D.T., Norfolk d.o.b. c.1910
Marsh dock	Roots made into ointment for measles, rashes, sunburn, dermatitis		Mrs F., Norfolk d.o.b. c.1935
	Ointment for burns		Mr J.B., Essex d.o.b. c.1925

Name of Plant	Remedy	Recorded by Taylor, 1920	Recorded by Hatfield 1990
Marshmallow (*Althaea officinalis L.*)	Root with honey for gargle		Sculthorpe Sch.
Meadowsweet (*Filipendula ulmaria (L.) Maxim*)	Infusion to relieve sunburn and freckles		Bircham WI
Milkweed (*Polygala vulgaris L.*)	Juice for warts		Several records e.g. Bircham WI
	Infusion to increase milk in nursing mothers		Mrs S.I., Norfolk d.o.b. c.1940
Mint (*Mentha sp*)	With ginger, for stomach trouble		Mr F.C. W., Norfolk d.o.b. c.1910
Mistletoe (*Viscum Album L.*)	For whooping cough		Mr R., Norfolk d.o.b. c.1900
	Leaf soaked overnight in milk, liquid drunk to prevent strokes		Mrs D.W., Essex d.o.b. c.1945
Mullein (*Verbascum thaspus*)	Infusion for coughs		Mrs S.I., Norfolk d.o.b. c.1940
Mushroom (*Agaricus campestris*)	Milk in which mushrooms have been boiled used to soothe cancer of oesophagus		Mrs H., Norfolk d.o.b. c.1900
Marigold (*Calendula officinalis L.*)	Infusion of flowers drunk for measles		Mr J.B., Essex d.o.b. c.1935

Name of Plant	Remedy	Recorded by Taylor, 1920	Recorded by Hatfield 1990
Marigold (*cont.*)	Juice from leaves for spots and impetigo		Mrs S.I., Norfolk d.o.b. c.1940
Nettle (*Urtica dioica L.*)	Juice from stalk for nettle sting	Dr B., Suffolk	
	Tea for 'spring humours'	Mr J., Rochford	
	Infusion 'good for blood'		Several records e.g. Lions Centre, Essex
	Dried and fed as tonic to goats, pigs, rabbits etc.		Mr M.C., Norfolk d.o.b. c.1935
	Infusion of young tops drunk for arthritis		Mrs I.H., Norfolk d.o.b. c.1930
	Infusion for high blood pressure		Mrs V.C., Essex d.o.b. c.1935
	To ensure pregnancy in mare, beat with nettles after she has been served		Mr J.C., Norfolk d.o.b. 1900
Oak	Bark boiled, drink liquor for rheumatism		Mrs L.B., Essex d.o.b. c.1935
	Acorn carried for rheumatism		Mr R.H., Suffolk d.o.b. c.1910
	Acorn grated in warm milk for diarrhoea	Woolverstone WI	
Onion (*Allium cepa L.*)	Hot Poultice for chest cold	Eyke WI	
	Outer skin for cracked lips	Bealings WI	
	Kernal of onion in cavity of sore tooth	Dr N., Huntingdon	

Name of Plant	Remedy	Recorded by Taylor, 1920	Recorded by Hatfield 1990
Onion (*cont.*)	Roast onion inserted into sore ear		Numerous records e.g. Mrs J., Norfolk d.o.b. c.1910
	Carried and eaten to ward off infection		Mrs B., Norfolk d.o.b. c.1930
	Poultice for earache and poultice for boils		Mrs P., Norfolk d.o.b. 1900
	Raw onion rubbed onto burns		Mr G., Norfolk d.o.b. 1900
	Raw onion rubbed on stings		Numerous records e.g. Toftwood Sch.
	Boiled for colds		Numerous records e.g. Alderman Peel Sch.
	With lemon and sugar, or with honey and vinegar, for coughs		
	Fumes inhaled, or juice drunk for whooping cough		Numerous records e.g. Alderman PeelSch.
	Rubbed on chilblains		Mrs M., Essex d.o.b. 1917
	Boiled for constipation		Mrs S.I., Norfolk d.o.b. c.1940

Name of Plant	Remedy	Recorded by Taylor, 1920	Recorded by Hatfield 1990
Parsley (*Petroselinum crispum (Mill) Nym*)	Poultice for boils	Blythburgh WI	
	Infusion of leaves and stalks for bruises		Miss N., Norfolk d.o.b. c.1920
	Boil and drinnk liquid for a weal bladder		Mrs L.B., Essex d.o.b. c.1930
	Good for arthritis		Several records e.g. Docking School
Parsnip (*Pastinaca sativa*)	Juice in which parsnips have been boiled for whooping cough		Mrs J., Norfolk d.o.b. c.1935
Pennyroyal (*Mentha pulegium L.*)	Abortion	Mrs B., Norwich	Lions Centre, Essex
Peppermint (*Mentha x piperata*)	Hot infusion for influenza		Mrs I.H., Norfolk d.o.b. c.1930
Plantain (*Plantago sp*)	Leaf for sores and cuts	Mrs M., Wivenhoe	Mrs M.B, Norfolk d.o.b. c.1940
	Lumbago		Mr R., Norfolk d.o.b. c.1900
	Concoction of leaves for incontinence		Mr J.B., Essex d.o.b. c.1935
Plantain, ribwort (*Plantago lanceolata L.*)	Infusion of leaves for diarrhoea		Mrs S.I., Norfolk d.o.b. c.1940

Name of Plant	Remedy	Recorded by Taylor, 1920	Recorded by Hatfield 1990
Plum (*Prunus sp*)	Bark, with sloe and cherry barks, made into decoction for whooping cough		Mrs S.I., Norfolk d.o.b. c.1940
Poppy (*Papaver rhoeas L.*)	Infusion of poppieds for earache		Mrs S.I., Norfolk d.o.b. c.1940
	Seeds chewed for hangover		Mrs E., Norfolk d.o.b. 1950
Poppy Garden (*Papaver somniferum L.*)	Petals macerated in milk for fevers in babies		Mr F.C.W., Norfolk d.o.b. c.1910
Potato (*Solanum tuberosum*)	Raw potato scraped for burns	Eyke WI	
	Carried in pocket to prevent rheumatism		Mr D.E.B., Essex d.o.b. 1925
	Poultice for asthma		Mrs D.T., Norfolk d.o.b. c.1910
	Poultice for sore throat	Blythburgh WI	
Primrose (*Primula vulgaris Huds*)	Leaves with linseed oil for burns	Blythburgh WI	
(*Pulmonaria officinalis L.*)	Decoction for consumption	Mrs B.	
Ragwort (*Senecio jacobaea L.*)	For gripes in horses		Mr G., Norfolk d.o.b. c.1910

Name of Plant	Remedy	Recorded by Taylor, 1920	Recorded by Hatfield 1990
Red deadnettle (*Lamium purpureum L.*)	Chopped into egg and fed to turkeys for blackhead		Hoxne Circle, Suffolk
	Fed to chickens for 'gapes'		Mr M.C., Norfolk d.o.b. c.1940
	Infuse in wine, drink for piles		Mr J.B., Essex d.o.b. c.1925
Rhubarb (*Rheum rhaponticum*)	Leaves held on fevered brow		Mrs F.S., Norfolk d.o.b. c.1920
	Sliced root for constipation		Mrs E.H., Norfolk d.o.b. c.1905
Roses (*Rosa spp*)	Squeeze red roses and add sugar for coughs and spitting of blood	Huntingfield WI	
	Shoots fed to goat for upset stomach		Mr L.S., Norfolk d.o.b. c.1920
	With lavender, makes lotion for rashes		Mrs A., Norfolk d.o.b. c.1940
	Briar leaves bound round cuts		Mrs D.P., Essex d.o.b. c.1900
	Rose-hips minced and boiled, juice used to 'bring out' old coat of horse		Mr M.C., Norfolk d.o.b. c.1940
	Rose-hips carried to prevent piles		Mr D.E.B., Essex d.o.b. 1925

Name of Plant	Remedy	Recorded by Taylor, 1920	Recorded by Hatfield 1990
Rosemary (*Rosmarinus officinalis L.*)	Hot infusion for colds	Orford WI	
Rue (*Ruta graveolens L.*)	Infusion for scarlet fever	Wilby WI	
	Scouring in chickens		Mr J.C., Norfolk d.o.b. 1900
	As tonic for pheasants		Mr J.C., norfolk d.o.b. 1900
	Gapes in chickens		Mr G., Norfolk d.o.b. c.1910
	Tea as spring ronic		Mr F.C.W., Norfolk d.o.b. c.1910
Raspberry (*Rubus idaeus L.*)	Tea during pregnancy for easy delivery		Numerous records e.g. Mrs S., Essex d.o.b. 1914
Saffron (*Crocus sativus L.*)	Abortion	Mrs S.B.	
Sage (*Salvia officinalis L.*)	With lemon and honey for colds	Blythburgh WI Eyke WI	
	With lemon and honey for gargle	Mrs S.B.	
	Sage tea for sciatica		Mr E.C., Essex d.o.b. 1925
	Water in which sage has been boiled for bathing sunburn		Mr D.B., Essex d.o.b. 1925 Whissonsett Circle

Name of Plant	Remedy	Recorded by Taylor, 1920	Recorded by Hatfield 1990
Saint John's wort (*Hypericum sp*)	Bedsores	Dr W.H., Lincoln	
Samphire (*Salicornia sp*)	Made into green ointment for cracked hands		Mrs B., Norfolk d.o.b. c.1940
	Eaten as spring tonic		Mr F.C.W., Norfolk d.o.b. c.1910
Scabious (*Knautia arvensis* (L.) Coult)	Boil in water, sit over steam for piles		Mr J.B., Essex d.o.b. c.1925
Sea lettuce (*Porphyra sp*)	Stewed in sea water, applied as poultice to relieve arthritis in feet		Mrs A., Norfolk d.o.b. c.1940
Seaweed	For rheumatism		King's Lynn School
Senna (*Cassia senna L.*)	Smoke from burned leaves inhaled for toothache	Sproughton WI	
Shallots (*Allium sp*)	Roasted for a cold		Mr A., Norfolk d.o.b. c.1920
Shepherd's purse (*Capsella bursapastoris* (L.) Medic)	Infusion for heavy periods		Mrs D.W., Essex d.o.b. c.1945
Sloe (*Prunus spinosa*)	Juice of boiled sloes for gargle	Huntingfield WI	
Solomon's seal (*Polygonatum multiflorum* (L.) All)	Root crushed and rubbed on to spots on face		Mrs E.H., Norfolk d.o.b., c.1900

Name of Plant	Remedy	Recorded by Taylor, 1920	Recorded by Hatfield 1990
Solomon's seal (*cont.*)	Made into ointment for ulcers and wounds in horses and cattle		Mr F.W., Norfolk d.o.b. c.1910
Spurge (*Euphorbia sp*)	Juice applied to warts		Mr F.W., Norfolk d.o.b. c.1910 and Mrs H., Essex d.o.b. c.1925
Stonecrop (*Sedum acre*)	Juice for dermatitis		Mrs P.B., Norfolk d.o.b. c.1935
Strawberry (*Fragaria vesca L.*)	Infusion of roots or leaves for rheumatism		Terrington St School
	Infusion of root, leaf or fruit for diarrhoea		Terrington St School
Sugar beet (*Beta vulgaris subsp cicla*)	Leaves fed to pigs for erysipelas		Hoxne Circle, Suffolk
Swede turnip (*Brassica napus var napobrassica*)	Sliced, sprinkled with brown suger, juice used as cough syrup		Terrington St Clem School and numerous other records
Tansy (*Tanacetum vulgare L.*)	Infusion of flowers or leaves for threadworms	Dr B., Lincoln	
	Used for period pains		Mrs B., Norfolk d.o.b. c.1935

Name of Plant	Remedy	Recorded by Taylor, 1920	Recorded by Hatfield 1990
Thorn apple (*Datura stramonium L.*)	Fruit boiled in pork grease for inflammations, burns, scalds		Mr F.C.W., Norfolk d.o.b. c.1910
	Top of fruit cut off, inside pulped, vinegar added. Inhale fumes for pain relief		Mr J.B., Essex d.o.b. c.1925
	Leaves smoked for asthma		Mr T.E., Norfolk d.o.b. c.1915 also King's Lynn School
Tobacco (*Nicotiana Tabacum L.*)	Strong infusion to destroy fleas on dogs	Mrs B., Norwich	
	Prevention of distemper in dogs	Dr P., North Walsham	
	Chew and rub on stings		Mr R.C., Norfolk d.o.b. c.1925
Turnip (*Brassica rapa*)	Raw, for poultices	Dr C.S.	
Valerian (*Valeriana officinalis L.*)	With garlic and skullcap for distemper in dogs		Miss R.N., Norfolk d.o.b. c.1920
Vervain (*Verbena officinalis L.*)	Infusion of leaves for sunburn		Mrs I.H., Norfolk d.o.b. c.1920
Vetches (*Vicia spp*)	Fed with oats to horses to keep blood cool		Mr M.C., Norfolk d.o.b. c.1935
Watercress (*Coronopus squamatus*)	Rub on red, swollen, inflamed eyelids		Mr R.C., Norfolk d.o.b. c.1925

Name of Plant	Remedy	Recorded by Taylor, 1920	Recorded by Hatfield 1990
Wheat (*Triticum aestivum*)	Oil of wheat for gastritis		Mr F.C.W., Norfolk d.o.b. c.1910
White deadnettle (*Lamium album L.*)	Infusion for skin conditions		Miss R.N., Norfolk d.o.b. c.1920
	Water in which deadnettles have been boiled drunk for arthritis	Cringleford WI	
White lily, madonna lily (*Lilium candidum L.*)	Flowers steeped in brandy for cuts	Yoxford WI, Eyke WI	Numerous records e.g. Mrs B.G., Essex d.o.b. 1912
	Leaves used likewise for cuts and boils		Mrs J., Essex d.o.b. c.1925
Willow (*Salix sp*)	Bark chewed for headache		Mr T.C., Essex d.o.b. 1918 Mr J., Lincs d.o.b. c.1950
	Bark in vinegar for corns		Mr F.C.W., Norfolk d.o.b. c.1910
	Bark for arthritis		King's Lynn School

Name of Plant	Remedy	Recorded by Taylor, 1920	Recorded by Hatfield 1990
Wormwood (*Artemisia absithium*)	Dried and infused for lumbago and rheumatism		Mrs E.H., d.o.b. c.1900
	To rid house of fleas		Mr M.R., Suffolk d.o.b. c.1910
	Leaves boiled and liquid drunk to improve appetite		Mr D.B., Essex d.o.b. 1925
Yarrow (*Achillea millefolium L.*)	Infusion for bronchitis	Dr S., Yarmouth	Kenninghall School
	Tea for measles, fevers, flu		Mr J.B., Essex d.o.b. 1925
	Tea to cure depression		
	Infusion of roots for rheumatism		Mrs R., Norwich d.o.b. c.1930
	Fed to rabbits for scouring		Miss R.N., Norfolk d.o.b. c.1920
	Ointment from stems, leaves and roots for cuts and scratches		Mrs A.A., Norfolk d.o.b. c.1940
Yew (*Taxus Baccata L.*)	Sprigs of Yew Tree steeped in tea for kidneys	Ancaster, Lincs.	

LIST OF WORKS CITED

Armstrong, A., *The Farmworkers 1770–1980*, Batsford, 1988.

Baker, Margaret, *Folklore and Customs of Rural England*, David and Charles, 1974.

Baldry, George, *The Rabbit Skin Cap*, ed. Lilias Rider Haggard, Collins, 1950.

Benn, Ernest, *The Olio Cookery Book by L. Sykes*, London, 1928.

Blythe, R., *Akenfield*, Penguin, 1969.

Bracken, Henry, MD, *Farriery Improved*, 1789.

British Herbal Pharmacopoeia, British Herbal Medicine Association, 1974.

British Pharmaceutical Codex, 1923.

Britten, J. & Holland, R., *Dictionary of English Plant Names*, Trubner, 1878.

Brooke, J. & E., *Suffolk Prospect*, Faber & Faber, 1963.

Buchan, William, *Domestic Medicine*, 3rd edition, 1774.

Chamberlain, Mary, *Old Wives Tales*, Virago, 1981.

Crowther, M.A., *The Workhouse System, 1834–1929*, Methuen, 1983.

Dew, Walton, *A Dysshe of Norfolk Dumplings*, London, 1898, re-issued EP Publishing, 1973.

Dorson, Richard M., (ed.), *Folklore and Folklife: an Introduction*, Chicago, 1972.

East Anglian Magazine, June 1975.

East Anglian Magazine, Dec. 1975.

Emerson, *Pictures of East Anglian Life*, 1887.

Evans, George Ewart, *The Pattern under the Plough*, Faber & Faber, 1966.

Evans, George Ewart, *The Farm and the Village*, Faber & Faber, 1969.

Evans, George Ewart, *Where Beards Wag All*, Faber & Faber, 1970.

Glyde, John, *The Norfolk Garland*, Jarrold, 1872.

Grieve, Mrs M., *A Modern Herbal*, Cape, 1931.

Griggs, Barbara, *Green Pharmacy: A History of Herbal Medicine*, Jill Norman & Hobhouse Ltd, 1981.

Haggard, Lilias Rider, ed., *I Walked by Night*, Boydell Press, 1974.

Hall, M. Penelope, *The Social Services of Modern England*, Routledge & Kegan, 1952.

Harrison, S.G., et al., *The Oxford Book of Food Plants*, London, 1985.

Hoffman, David, *The Holistic Herbal*, Findhorn Press, 1983.

Harland, Elizabeth, *No Halt at Sunset: The Diary of a Country Housewife*, Benn, 1951.

Hawkins, C.B., *Norwich, A Social Study*, Philip Lee Warner, 1910.

Jobson, A., *Victorian Suffolk*, Hale, London, 1972.

Leyel, Mrs C.F., *The Magic of Herbs*, Jonathan Cape, London, 1926.

MacSelf, ed. *The Woman's Treasury for Home and Garden*, London, Amateur Gardening Offices, n.d.

More Secret Remedies, British Medical Association, London, 1912.

Pechey, John, *The Compleat Herbal of Physical Plants*, London, 1694.

Petch, C.P. & Swann, E.L., *Flora of Norfolk*, Jarrold, 1968.

Porter, Enid, 'Some Old Fenland Remedies', *Education Today*, July, 1964.

Porter, Enid, *The Folklore of East Anglia*, Batsford, 1974.

Potter's New Cyclopaedia of Botanical Drugs and Preparations, R.C. Wren, re-written by Williamson and Evans, 1988, C.W. Daniel Co. Ltd.

Report on the British Health Services, Dec. 1937, PEP, London.

R.C. Wren, *Potter's New Cyclopaedia of Botanical Drugs and Preparations*, Health Science Press, 1975.

Suffling, Ernest R., *History and Legends of the Broads District*, Jarrold, 1891.

The Herball or Generall Historie of Plantes, John Gerarde, The Essence thereof Distilled by Marcus Woodward from the Edition of Th.Johnson, 1636, Studio Editions, London, 1985.

The Poor Man's Physician or the Receits of the Famous John Moncrief of Tippermalloch, 33rd edition, Edinburgh, 1731.

Wheelwright, E.G., *The Physick Garden*, Cape, 1934.

Within Living Memory, Norfolk Federation of Women's Institutes, Boydell Press, 1973.

Young, J., *Farming in East Anglia*, David Rendel, London, 1967.

INDEX TO AILMENTS
AND COMMON NAMES OF PLANTS